5 Steps to Christlike Living

D1456797

Randy Maxwell

Edited by Jerry D. Thomas
Designed by Michelle C. Petz
Cover photos: Sky © PhotoDisc. Inc.
           Randy Maxwell © 2000 Ed Guthero

Copyright © 2001 by
Pacific Press® Publishing Association
Printed in the United States of America
All Rights Reserved

ISBN 0-8163-1816-6

01 02 03 04 05 • 5 4 3 2 1

Contents

Foreword

Prayer

1. 5 Steps to More Effective Prayer 9
2. 5 Ways to Pray for and With Children 14
3. 5 Ways to Connect With God Despite a Busy Schedule .. 20
4. 5 Reasons Why We Don't Need a Constitutional Amendment on Prayer 25

Spirituality

5. 5 Ways to Be a More Spiritual Person 33
6. 5 Ways to Restore Your Spiritual Passion 37
7. 5 Ways to Know God's Will for Your Life 41
8. 5 Ways to Grow Spiritually in the New Millennium 46
9. 5 Ways to Be Free in Jesus 51
10. 5 Ways to Increase Your Faith 56
11. 5 Ways to Deal With Guilt 61
12. 5 Ways to Overcome the Spiritual Blahs 66

Relationships

13. 5 Ways to Romance Your Spouse 73
14. 5 Ways to Live With an Unbelieving Spouse 77
15. 5 Ways to Live With a Believing Spouse 82
16. 5 Ways to Get Along With Your Teenager 87

Christian Living

17. 5 Steps to Salvation 93
18. 5 Tips for Getting More out of Church 98
19. 5 Things You Can Do to Support Your Pastor 103
20. 5 Ways to Reach Out to Members of a Different Ethnic Group 108
21. 5 Tips for Getting More out of Bible Study 113
22. 5 Reasons Why I Believe in God 118
23. 5 Ways to Stop Being Miserable 123

Foreword

Several years ago a group of pastors in California were asked to share some ideas about how to make *Signs of the Times®* a more effective magazine. One of their recommendations especially impressed us—that we publish articles with specific suggestions on *how* to live the spiritual life. Our entire editorial committee agreed that it was an excellent idea.

But how to implement it?

After considerable discussion, we settled on two important elements the project *must* have in order to succeed. First, we wanted a series of articles with a theme that was broad enough to encompass a wide variety of spiritual topics and that could run for one or two years. The theme we settled on was "Five Ways to . . . ." This theme could include everything from "Five Ways to Pray" to "Five Ways to Handle Your Anger with God."

Second, we decided that we needed a single author in order to ensure the quality and continuity of the series. We knew the series needed an author who could provide practical insights on spiritual themes, and of course we wanted a *good* writer. We considered several names, but in

Foreword

the end Randy Maxwell's name stood out above all the others.

Randy has become very well known for his books on prayer. He has conducted many seminars on prayer all across North America and in a number of foreign countries. Randy is also an experienced author who we knew could produce consistently good articles.

And so, from January 1998 through December 1999, the readers of *Signs of the Times*® were treated to 24 articles by Randy Maxwell on a wide variety of spiritual themes, all organized around the title "Five Ways to . . . ." Randy produced exactly the kind of articles we were looking for, and from the correspondence we received, we know that our *Signs* readers agreed.

Now these articles have been published as a book—the book you are holding in your hands. You will find each chapter to contain practical step-by-step guidelines for your life as a believer. Randy avoids fluffy philosophy and stained-glass theory in his writing. He speaks from the heart about the issues and challenges that confront flesh and blood Christians day in and day out in their walk with God. I can guarantee that you will enjoy Randy's winsome way of applying spiritual truths to everyday situations that impact our prayer life, relationships, and Christian growth.

In addition to the editor-author relationship Randy and I enjoy, we are plain good friends. I came to Pacific Press® as a book editor in December 1986, and Randy joined the publishing house as a book editor about a year later. So we've been friends the better part of 15 years. It's always a pleasure to hear Randy's hearty laugh in the halls of Pacific Press®!

I hope you'll give thoughtful attention to each of Randy's chapters, because I know you'll find in them a bit of the friendship I've enjoyed with him over the years. And I know that the spiritual purpose our editorial committee had for publishing Randy's articles in *Signs of the Times*® in the first place will be realized in your life.

Marvin Moore, editor
Signs of the Times®

Dedication

To Marvin.
Thanks for the opportunity.

PRAYER

Talking to God is one of our greatest privileges. Yet many Christians find prayer to be a perplexing exercise that often results in boredom, guilt, and frustration. The first three chapters in this section are intended to demystify the discipline of prayer and make it a joyful encounter with God that we can experience anytime, anywhere. The suggestions here are largely taken from my two books on prayer, *If My People Pray* and *Bring Back the Glory*.

The fourth chapter deals with the issue of a constitutional amendment on prayer. Because I'm an outspoken advocate of prayer, many may be surprised at my opinions on this hotly debated issue. But I pray the discussion will result in deeper thinking about what real prayer is, because prayer is foundational to Christlike living.

Steps to More Effective Prayer

Many of us view prayer the same way we do exercise. We know exercise is good for us. It relieves stress, improves the circulation, strengthens the heart, boosts the energy level, and improves physical appearance. Some claim that exercise even enhances one's sex life!

But despite these valid and desirable benefits, many of us would rather keep lifting a fork to our mouths than lift weights. Exercise is boring, painful, and just too much trouble after a hard day sitting on our spreading posteriors down at the air-conditioned office!

Similarly, deep down in our spirits, we know that prayer is important—that it strengthens our relationship with God, relieves stress, boosts our faith, and is the source of unlimited spiritual power. But despite these benefits, many of us view prayer as boring, painful, and just too much trouble.

So how do we shake ourselves out of the doldrums and really begin to experience intimate fellowship with God in prayer?

5 Steps to Christlike Living

1. PRAY WHENEVER YOU THINK ABOUT PRAYING.

Don't make the mistake of thinking you can only pray at certain times and in certain places. Pray in your car, in a meeting, in bed when you can't sleep, as you mow the lawn or wash dishes, or while brushing your teeth.

Learn this if you learn nothing else: Because God makes His home in you,[1] *wherever you are, God is!* So learn to converse with Him all the time.

I used to—and occasionally still do—fall into the trap of telling myself "I'll pray about that later." While I'm mowing the lawn I'll think of someone I need to pray for. I'll mentally review the details of that person's need and even rehearse what I plan to say *later*, during my "prayer time." Then I catch myself and smile at how foolish it is for me to pray later about something I'm thinking (and actually praying) about *now!*

If you sometimes find yourself kicking yourself for forgetting to pray for people you've promised to pray for, learn to pray when God puts the burden on your mind—when you think about it.

2. PRAY ABOUT A VARIETY OF THINGS.

Don't pray about the same things all the time, and don't try to cover everything in one prayer. Vary your conversation. Pray today about the supervisor who is giving you grief and save the missionaries for tomorrow.

Pray different types of prayers. Try praying a prayer of praise without any petitions. Make no requests about anything. Put away the shopping list and just spend time praising God for who He is in your life.

Or sing your prayer to God. Paul admonishes us to "sing psalms, hymns, and spiritual songs with gratitude in your hearts to God."[2] There are times when my family and I pray by singing favorite praise hymns such as "Great Is Thy Faithfulness" and "I Love You, Lord."

During sung prayers, I sometimes experience the presence of God more profoundly than when I'm at my "regular" prayers.

3. PRAY WITHOUT WORDS.

You don't always have to have something to say in order to be with God. I know this may seem odd, but sometimes it's perfectly all right "to be still, and know that [He is] God."[3]

One morning not long ago, I had a deeply moving encounter with God without saying a word. It was one of those extremely rare times when both the house and my spirit were quiet. I couldn't think of anything to read or anything to say. I sat in the stillness and just allowed my heart to be an open book to God.

I noted the experience in my journal later that morning:

> The stillness of this morning feels good—like a warm blanket on a cold night. I seem unable—or unwilling—to think of a passage to read from the Bible. I'm not in a hurry to read anything. For now, the silence is enough. My thoughts and the quiet seem prayer enough this morning. "Be still [cease striving] and know that I am God," You've said. This is one of those rare moments when I'm content to sit still and know You. To connect with the King. Thank You for meeting me here this morning.

Learn to "be still and know." Quiet can be profound. And don't feel as if you've failed if you occasionally run out of words when you pray. Remember, there are times when "we do not know what we ought to pray for, but the Spirit himself intercedes for us with groans that words cannot express. And he who searches our hearts knows the mind of the Spirit, because the Spirit intercedes for the saints in accordance with God's will."[4]

4. PRAY ON PAPER.

Prayer journaling is simply writing your prayer in the form of a letter to God. It is also one of the best methods I know for dealing with a wandering mind. When I'm writing my thoughts to God, I find that my mind stays focused on what I'm writing. My eyes are open, and there's something in my hand that keeps me alert. And I often hear God speaking back to me as I write in my journal. God addresses the very issue I'm writing about—not audibly but in my mind, through a scripture, a remembered circumstance, a song.

Don't worry about proper grammar or punctuation. Your journal is for God's eyes only. It isn't meant for publication in *Signs of the Times*®! Buy a simple spiral notebook, date the top of the page, and begin to express yourself on paper.

Journaling is a powerful way to communicate with God—and, as a bonus, you'll have a permanent record of your spiritual journey with God. Years from now you'll look back at your prayer journal to see how God led you through times of struggle; it will give you courage to face the challenges of tomorrow.

5. PRAY FOR YOUR SPOUSE.

Don't pray in a general, vague way but in specific terms, claiming particular Bible promises that are tailored to your spouse's individual needs.

I like to do this for my wife, Suzette. Sometimes I'll leave her a note containing the verse that I'm claiming for her. She saved one of these notes and kept it for a time on the bathroom mirror, where she could see it every day. It read:

> For you today: That your delight will be in the law of the Lord, that you will meditate on it day and night. That you will be like a tree planted by streams of water, yielding fruit in season without withering. And that whatever you do will prosper (Psalm 1:2, 3). Love ya.

Search the Word for specific verses that fit your spouse's situation and pray those verses back to God, inserting your husband's or wife's name in the appropriate place.

P.S. You can pray for your children the same way.

And singles, the lack of a spouse and children doesn't mean the lack of other individuals who love you and need your prayers. Claim promises on behalf of your best friend, co-worker, family member, or pastor, and let that person know that you are praying for him or her. Any relationship will be strengthened by this prayerful act of love.

So there you have it. Five suggestions for putting new passion into your personal prayer journey with God. Not an exhaustive list by any stretch. You may already be experimenting with several creative forms of prayer that aren't even mentioned here. Great. Go for it. Whatever you do, though, *pray*.

Don't just read about prayer or agree that it's important. *Pray*.

Be real. Be consistent. Be creative. But above all, *pray*.

There's so much in store for you if you do.

---

1. See John 14:23; 1 Corinthians 6:19.

2. Colossians 3:16.

3. Psalm 46:10.

4. Romans 8:26, 27.

This chapter is adapted from Randy's book, If My People Pray, *Pacific Press® Publishing Association, Boise, Idaho, 1995.*

Ways to Pray for and With Children

Recently, one of our local Christian radio stations, KTSY, had a prayer and praise day. For 12 hours straight, the phone lines were open, and listeners could call and praise God for an answered prayer and also make prayer requests. During one segment of the day, listeners were invited to call in and nominate someone for the faith hall of fame—someone whom they felt demonstrated faith by the way they lived. One little boy called in and nominated his mom. When the announcer asked this youngster why his mother should be in the faith hall of fame, he answered, "Because my mom prays for me every day."

How I wish this was the proud boast of every child! At the risk of offending those of my own generation, I have to say that on the whole, we've done a lousy job of parenting. Determined not to grow up, and mired in materialistic self-indulgence, Boomers have neglected their children, spoiled them, modeled alcohol and drug use in front of them, and failed to provide the moral boundaries that teach them what is right and wrong.

I realize this is a generalization. Of course there are exceptions. Many of us provide computers and private-school education for our children to give them a head start on a successful adulthood. But of all the things we do for our children, prayer is most important.

Why pray for our children? Because Satan wants them. Jesus told Peter, "Satan has asked to sift you as wheat,"[1] and this is what the enemy wants to do to our children in these last days.

The evidences that our children are being "sifted" by the enemy and stand in need of our prayers more than ever are abundant. Consider the following.

• September 1995—A family makes a wrong turn down a street in Los Angeles and gets trapped in a hail of gunfire that kills their little girl. Gang members pour bullets into the car for the fun of it.

• November 1996—A teenage girl gives birth in a Delaware motel, then she and her boyfriend allegedly beat the child to death, place it in a plastic bag, and drop it in a dumpster.

• June 1997—A New Jersey teen gives birth to a baby in a bathroom stall at her high-school prom. She drops the baby in the trash, then returns to the dance floor.

• October 1997—A 16-year-old boy in Pearl, Mississippi, guns down his mother and then goes to school and shoots nine students, killing two, including his former girlfriend.

• December 1997—A young boy opens fire on a prayer meeting at Heath High School in Paducah, Kentucky, killing three and wounding five of his classmates.

• March 1998—A 13- and an 11-year-old gun down four students and a teacher in Jonesboro, Arkansas.

• April 1998—In Yonkers, New York, a 15-year-old girl, upset that her teacher called her parents about her poor academic performance, attacked the pregnant teacher with a hammer.

But we are not helpless in this struggle for the souls of our children. We must fight! Lamentations 2:19 gives us our battle plan: "Pour out your heart like water in the presence of the Lord. Lift up your hands to him for the lives of your children."

At this point in our discussion, I need to say something very important. *Strive to be a praying parent, not a perfect parent.* It's not being a perfect parent that makes the difference in a child's life. None of us are perfect, so how can we be perfect parents? It's the *praying* parent that makes the difference. And that's something we *all* can be.

Here are five ways we can pray for and with our children.

1. PRAY A PRAYER OF BLESSING ON YOUR CHILDREN.[2]

How important it is that our children receive God's blessing! Our kids hunger to know that they are special, that there's no one else who owns the key to our hearts in exactly the same way. And they hunger to know that God is their Friend and that His smile, not His frown, is on them. We have the incredible privilege as parents and New Testament priests[3] to administer blessing to our children.

Call your children to your side at least once a year—perhaps on their birthdays or on New Year's Eve. Place your hands upon their heads, representing God's hands of provision and protection. Thank God for each unique child of yours, and then, inserting his or her name in the text, repeat the words of blessing found in Numbers 6:24, 25:

> "The Lord bless you and keep you; the Lord make His face shine upon you, and be gracious to you; The Lord lift up His countenance upon you, and give you peace."[4]

Parents, don't miss out on one of your highest privileges—that of blessing your children. You don't have to do it exactly as described above, but find your way to communicate God's approval and delight in your sons and daughters, be they four, fourteen, or forty! And do you know what? God promises to put His name on your children and to bless them.[5] What more could you want for them?

2. MAKE PERSONALIZED PRAYER LISTS FOR EACH CHILD.

The credit for this idea goes to Stormie Omartian, author of *The Power of a Praying Parent.*[6] Designate a time each year, perhaps at the beginning of summer vacation, to make a prayer list for each of your children. Take pencil and paper in hand, and ask God to show you how to pray for each child over the next twelve months. Claim Psalm 25:14 as you do this, believing that He will reveal your children's needs to you when you ask.

This exercise may take several days. Feel free to add to the lists as needed throughout the year.

3. PRAY, CLAIMING PROMISES FROM SCRIPTURE.

To the list you created in step two, add gifts, and claim the associated Scripture verses:

A. Protection—Psalm 17:8, 9; 91:1, 2, 9, 10-12; Isaiah 54:17.

B. Love and acceptance—Isaiah 41:9; Jeremiah 31:3; Romans 5:8.

C. Respect for parents and other authorities—Proverbs 1:8, 9; Isaiah 30:1; Ephesians 6:1-3; Colossians 3:20.

D. Godly friends and role models—Psalm 1:1; Proverbs 4:14; 12:26; 22:24, 25.

E. A hunger for the things of God—Psalm 86:11, 12; 119:2; Proverbs 14:27; Matthew 5:6.

F. Recognition of God-given gifts and talents—Proverbs 18:6; 22:29; Romans 11:29; 1 Peter 4:10.

G. Freedom from fear—Psalm 27:1; 34:4; Isaiah 41:10; 2 Timothy 1:7; 1 John 4:18.

H. A sound mind—Romans 12:2; 2 Corinthians 10:4, 5; Ephesians 4:17, 18, 22-24; Philippians 2:5; 4:8; 2 Timothy 1:7.

I. Freedom from alcohol, drugs, and other addictions—Deuteronomy 30:19; John 8:36; Romans 8:13.

J. Sexual purity—1 Corinthians 6:13, 18; 10:13; 1 Thessalonians 4:3-5; James 1:12; 1 Peter 2:11.

5 Steps to Christlike Living

> K. The right mate— Psalm 127:1; Proverbs 3:5, 6; 18:22; Malachi 2:13-16; Hebrews 13:4.

4. MAKE IT REAL.

Children do what they see. If prayer is to be real to them, it must first be real to their parents. So model time alone with Jesus. Let your children "catch" you on your knees during times of private prayer and devotion. In this way, they'll see that prayer is important to Mom or Dad.

Pray after the TV news. This will bring a sense of reality to prayer. Prayer becomes relevant when you make the real-life problems you've seen the subject of your talks with God.

Don't fuss when your children don't feel like praying. Pray for them aloud during those times, and give them space as they develop their relationship with God. A forced prayer through pouting lips and tear-streaked cheeks won't benefit anyone. Don't saddle prayer with negative pressure to perform.

5. MAKE IT SIMPLE AND FUN.

Keep prayer with the children simple and short. Teach them to be as specific as possible, and let them know that it is appropriate to pray anytime and anywhere. Use creative approaches to prayer, like "prayer balloons." Write your prayer requests on slips of paper, insert them into uninflated balloons, and fill the balloons with helium. When released, the balloons become a visual object lesson teaching that our prayers ascend to God.

In our home, we enjoy creating "prayer stars." Everyone kneels in a circle on the carpet with our folded hands touching at the fingertips. When we finish praying, we drop our still-folded-and-touching hands to the carpet, and then everyone leans back, pulling their hands apart in a v-shape along the carpet. The result is a starburst pattern on the carpet—a visible mark on the spot where we had family prayer.

Place prayer or Scripture verses in your children's lunch pails so that when they open them around noontime, they'll know that you're thinking and praying about them.

PRAYER

These are just a few of the ways to make prayer an important part of your children's lives. Experiment. Be bold and creative. Just remember that of all the things we do for our children, prayer is most important. It may be the thing that gets you a nomination into the "faith hall of fame" from a grateful child—and from Jesus, who prays for you without ceasing.[7]

---

1. Luke 22:31.
2. Numbers 6:22-27.
3. 1 Peter 2:9.
4. NKJV.
5. See Numbers 6:27.
6. Eugene, Oregon: Harvest House Publishers, 1995.
7. Hebrews 7:25.

Ways to Connect With God Despite a Busy Schedule

My kids are fans of those cute, animated vegetables who star in the wildly popular VeggieTales® video series. Episode three presents The Story of Flibber-O-Loo, a creative adaptation of Jesus' parable of the good Samaritan. Larry the Cucumber encounters bullies who steal his lunch money and leave him upside down in a hole. Along comes the mayor of Flibber-O-Loo, Larry's home town. When the victimized cucumber asks for help, the mayor (an asparagus with a British accent) sings this little song:

> I'm busy, busy, dreadfully busy,
> you've no idea what I have to do.
> Busy, busy, shockingly busy,
> *much, much too busy for you.*

Sound familiar?

Our lives are very much like this simple song. We're all dreadfully, shockingly busy. Major life events come and go with the speed of a mouse click on the computer. Graduations, basketball practice, braces, business trips, doctor visits, car trouble, grocery shopping, overdue library books, church duties, shuttling kids back and forth to school, lunches to fix, shots for the dog, magazine or book deadlines, jury duty, piano lessons, unexpected house guests, unexpected illnesses, job changes, etc., etc. The demands on our time are incessant and irrational. Solitude is a fantasy.

And somewhere in the scattered mess that is our lives, there is supposed to be time for holiness. Time to get deep with God. Time to pursue and experience spiritual renewal. How? How can we—with our cell phones, web pages, Palm Pilots, pagers, and 500-channel, high-definition TV sets—ever have the time or energy to connect with God in a way that produces true spiritual growth and depth? I'm still working this out for myself, but here are five things that can help get us out of the rat race and into God's presence:

1. GET SOME SLEEP.

Recent national surveys reveal that millions of Americans are terribly sleep deprived. Forty percent of adults say that they are so sleepy during the day that it interferes with their daily activities.[1] Maybe you're like my wife. She's on the go from the time her feet hit the floor in the morning until her head hits the pillow at night (usually around midnight!). She spins and spins, never allowing herself time to stop. But the moment she sits or lays down, she's fast asleep. When you're that tired, it's nearly impossible to have a productive "quiet time" in prayer and in God's Word. Thirty seconds into your Bible reading, and the words start runningtogetherinablobandbeforeyouknowityou'reasleeeeeeee . . .

Follow Elijah's example—get some sleep. After a big day on Mt. Carmel—praying fire and rain down from heaven, killing the prophets of Baal, and running faster than Ahab's chariot all the way to Jezreel—Elijah got word that Jezebel had taken out a contract on his life. He then ran "a day's journey into the desert" to escape the queen. There, exhausted and depressed, this mighty man of God prayed for death and then "fell asleep."[2]

Read the story carefully, and you'll see that God didn't chastise Elijah

5 Steps to Christlike Living

for his depression or his suicidal prayer. He knew that Elijah needed rest. We need it too. Start paying attention to your sleep habits. Stick to a regular schedule for going to bed and waking up, even on weekends. Give yourself permission to lie down and get some rest. If you're refreshed and alert, your mind and spirit will be receptive to the voice of God.

2. LEARN TO SAY NO.

This is a tough one for me. However, my wife says that since I turned 40 last year, I've improved—I say No more often. (She even told me to practice saying it in front of the mirror!) I'm not advocating the wholesale abandonment of all your duties, but I am urging that you use greater discretion. How many things are you currently doing only out of fear of disappointing others or fear of not being needed? How many of your current activities do you secretly resent? Pray for and exercise discernment—that spiritual ability to choose what is best over what is merely good. Saying No is an effective means of decluttering your life. You'll have more time to slow down, to be alone, pour out your overburdened heart to God, and admit your desperate need for inner refreshment.

3. BE QUIET.

I can't say this strongly enough. *Silence is indispensable if we hope to add depth to our spiritual life.* In his book *Intimacy With the Almighty,* Charles Swindoll writes, "Noise and words and frenzied, hectic schedules dull our senses, closing our ears to His still, small voice and making us numb to His touch."[3]

Last summer our family spent a few hours in Utah's Zion National Park. We oohed and aahed at the magnificent red rock formations that towered above us. But it was the silence combined with the visual spectacle that made us feel God's awesome presence. Three hours down I-15 we were in Las Vegas. Talk about a contrast! It was easy to see how the still, small voice of God would be difficult to hear amid the orgy of noise, pleasure seeking, and sensory stimulation of that place.

You can't control the noise of the world around you, but you can turn down the volume of your own inner space. Make room for quiet in your life. Unplug the phone. Shut off the TV. Turn off the radio or CD player, and spend some time every day in silence.

I won't kid you. This will be very difficult to do. As I write these words, I'm all alone in my living room, but the washing machine is chugging away in the laundry room next door, and the sounds of my kids' *Adventure in Odyssey* tapes are floating down the hall. It's hard to filter out the noise. However, we must try, for intimacy is best developed in silence where distractions are reduced and we can focus our full attention on God.

4. SEIZE THE "GOD MOMENTS."

I heard a preacher say that when you're really hungry for God, you can hear His voice even in a conversation between two people on a bus! Here's the point: Look and listen for God in the most routine aspects of your day. He's there. Even as the disciples gathered up the fragments left over from the meal of fishes and loaves,[4] we can gather fragments of time and use them to connect with God. Sing or pray while you drive. While brushing your teeth, memorize a scripture verse that you've written on an index card or Post-it® note and stuck on the bathroom mirror. As you pull weeds from your garden, tell your kids about the "weeds" of sin. When the alarm shatters your sleep tomorrow morning, breathe a 20-second prayer of commitment to the Lord before hitting the shower or the snooze button. Look for and encounter God throughout your day, and you'll remain connected to Him despite the busyness.

5. WORSHIP.

Take a whole day off for worship. That's right—a whole day. You may think I'm crazy for suggesting this, but it isn't my idea. It's God's. In fact, He thought it important enough to make it one of His Ten Commandments (see Exodus 20:8-11). God knew that, left to our own devices, we'd work ourselves to death and forget about Him in the process. He also knew that to grow and deepen, relationships must have *time.*

5 Steps to Christlike Living

Keeping the Sabbath holy is an amazing privilege and restorative practice that I enjoy every week. When sunset rolls around on Friday evening,[5] the TVs and newspapers get the day off, and the Maxwell family gathers for prayer and praises to the Creator who made and redeemed us. We spend the next 24 hours in corporate worship, rest, family time, and getting out in nature without the distractions that jangle our nerves and bombard our every waking moment on the other days of the week.

Shallowness is the bane of our times. Depth of Christian experience can be ours if we will begin putting our inner worlds in order and doing things God's way. And if we do so, God will give us a new song to sing in place of the one sung by the mayor of Flibber-O-Loo.

" 'In repentance and rest is your salvation, in quietness and trust is your strength.' "[6]

---

1. "How Sleepy Are You? 1999 U.S. Sleep Survey Shows Disturbing Trends in Daytime Sleepiness," <www.sleepfoundation.org/PressArchives/lead.html>.

2. 1Kings 19:5.

3. Charles Swindoll, *Intimacy With the Almighty*, (Dallas, Tex.: Word, 1996), 38, 39.

4. See Mark 6:43.

5. The biblical Sabbath, established at Creation, is celebrated from sunset to sunset, or "from even unto even" (Leviticus 23:32, KJV; cp. Mark 1:32). Proclaimed "holy" by God (Genesis 2:3; Exodus 20:8; Leviticus 23:3; Isaiah 58:13, 14), the Sabbath is more than a "holiday" from work. It is sacred time set apart for humans (Mark 2:27) to worship (Luke 4:16), to bless others (Matthew 12:11,12), and to "remember" Whose we are, Who we serve, and Who enables our lives (Exodus 20:11).

6. Isaiah 30:15.

Reasons Why We Don't Need a Constitutional Amendment on Prayer

By the time you read this, years will have passed since that fateful day when two trench coat–clad teens managed to shock even this violence-hardened nation with the murders of 12 classmates, a teacher, and finally themselves. The growing list of bloody school shootings is beginning to take a toll on our national psyche. Like the USS *Arizona,* the Tomb of the Unknown Soldier, and the Vietnam War Memorial, the names Moses Lake, Pearl, Paducah, Jonesboro, Springfield, Littleton, and Conyers evoke feelings of inconsolable loss.

The violence has led to a blame game of astronomical proportions. Parents, video games, Hollywood, access to guns, music, and eroding moral values are among the most popular targets. Solutions range from gun control to armed guards in schools to a constitutional amendment returning prayer to the classroom. And here is where many people of faith become very passionate. Many of them see the schoolyard carnage as a symptom of moral decline that began with the 1962 Supreme Court *Engel* decision[1]—a ruling that has prompted many Christians to accuse the high court of "kicking God out of our public schools." For those

5 Steps to Christlike Living

who see the world through these glasses, the formula for fixing what is broken in our nation is simple:

> Prayer out = violence in
> Prayer in = violence out

So it came as no surprise to me the day I received the following letter:

> WAKE UP AMERICA!!! Remember Jonesboro—Remember West Memphis. The children are not to blame, it is us, we the people. We let PRAYER be taken out of our schools. TV teaches violence. We need 25,000,000 (twenty-five million) signatures to have the Constitution amended to put prayer back in our schools. You may help by copying this form. Have your friends sign it and then mail it to . . .

You might expect every Christian who loves God and country to race for their ink pens to sign this petition, right? Wrong. I love my God and my country, but I'm *not* signing. Why not? Doesn't Randy Maxwell believe in prayer? Anyone who knows me knows that I believe in and encourage prayer. I conduct prayer conferences across the country and have written books on prayer and revival.[2] So why wouldn't I support a constitutional amendment to return prayer to our public schools? Here are my five reasons:

1. PRAYER IS ALREADY IN OUR SCHOOLS.

That's right. TV news reports the killings, but it doesn't always report the praying. Did you know that one out of every four public schools in the country has a "club" where Bible study and prayer are center stage? David Van Biema reports, " 'Once a religious scorched-earth zone, the schoolyard is suddenly fertile ground for both Vine and Branches.' "[3]

Van Biema says that the prayer group in West Paducah, Kentucky, which lost four of its members to automatic weapons fired by a fellow student while they prayed, has grown from 35 to nearly 150. He concludes, " 'For now the prospects for prayer clubs seem unlimited.' "

Contrary to popular opinion, the Supreme Court did *not* rule against voluntary prayer in public schools. The *Engel* case simply ruled that the regents of New York had no business composing an official prayer to be recited by students in its public school system. "Students could write a prayer—but they can do that under current law. So can their pastors. Nothing in the *Engel* decision precludes a clergyman writing a prayer, passing it on to his junior members, and asking them to pray it during the school day. So long as they don't disrupt the classroom in doing so, they are free to pray away."[4]

And praying they are. Van Biema reports on the outbreak of revival on *public school campuses* in the wake of the Columbine High shootings:

> The enthusiasm caps a decade of extraordinary growth for Christian youth groups in middle and high schools. The U.S. Supreme Court in 1990 upheld a law effectively allowing prayer clubs to meet on public school property if they did so outside of class hours and without adult supervision. Since then, thousands of Bible and prayer clubs have whooshed into what their members saw as a God-shaped vacuum.[5]

We don't need a constitutional amendment for a freedom we already have.

2. PRAYER NEEDS TO BE IN OUR CHURCHES AND HOMES FIRST.

I agree with Pastor Jim Cymbala of the renowned Brooklyn Tabernacle when he says that he's embarrassed by religious leaders who call for prayer in public schools when they don't even have prayer in the churches. For many, prayer meeting is a relic of a bygone era. Today, if there isn't some superstar preacher or hot music act, people stay home and watch television.

5 Steps to Christlike Living

Baptist preacher Greg Brooks has this to say: "Calls for reinstating prayer in the public schools are an indictment of the church. *Turning to government for assistance in propagating the faith is an unconscious admission that the church has failed.* Because we have not been agents of social change, we want government (in the form of public schools) to do our job for us, even though it's not the government's job to convert people to Christ, nor is it the school's job to promote religion."[6]

The church and the family are the primary avenues for propagating the gospel of Jesus Christ. We can't cast stones at the secular arena when our glass houses of worship are so vulnerable. If we make sure prayer is taking place in our homes and churches, we'll succeed in passing spiritual values to the next generation—without government's aid.

3. MANDATED PRAYER IS NOT REAL PRAYER.

Real prayer comes from the heart; it is not coerced. It is communing with God as with a friend. Mandated periods of "silence" and pre-written prayers don't meet this criteria. They tend to trivialize rather than bolster genuine faith. Again, Pastor Brooks states:

> Religion also suffers by any attempt to prop itself up through governmental sanction, the idea being that religious faith and practices are legitimized when officially recognized. What really happens, however, is that instead of being legitimized, the religious practices are trivialized. . . . Indeed, prayers designed to be 'non-offensive' and 'nonsectarian' end up being generic, bland, meaningless incantations 'to whom it may concern'—hardly the stuff that could have the kind of impact on lives that would reverse America's moral decline.[7]

Force-fed religion makes no one holy. Remember, fourteen-year-old Michael Carneal opened fire on a student prayer meeting. Prayer at the school didn't stop him. Evil does exist in this world, and a generic prayer recited at the beginning of the day would not have stopped Michael or Kip or Eric or Dylan.

4. MANDATED PRAYER CANNOT ATONE FOR UNINVOLVED PARENTS.

I recently participated as a judge in an essay contest for 7th through 12th graders on the subject of drugs, role models, and choices. The Columbine shootings were still very fresh, and that fact was reflected in the writings of these young citizens. One recurring theme emerged loud and clear from the essays—*kids want their parents' time and attention.* No government-structured prayer can make up for parental neglect.

Listen to your kids. Pray with them. Set some standards for them, and discipline them—*please.* This was the message I got over and over again as I read essay after essay. Our children are begging for loving boundaries, not Beemers. Let's give them real love.

5. MANDATED PRAYER THREATENS OUR RELIGIOUS FREEDOMS.

It was James Madison, author of the First Amendment, who said: "It is proper to take alarm at the first experiment on our liberties. . . . Who does not see that the same authority which can establish Christianity, in exclusion of all other religions, may establish with the same ease any particular sect of Christians, in exclusion of all other sects?"

Many of the readers of this column are politically conservative and oppose government intrusion into our lives. If you resist gun control, shouldn't you resist prayer control as well? Let government do what it does, and let the church of Christ do the work of preaching the gospel. We can save our children without government help. In fact, if we follow the examples of young people like Littleton martyr Cassie Bernall and countless Christian teens who are voluntarily living their faith on public school campuses, maybe our churches and then our nation will be next to experience revival.

---

1. The *Engel vs. Vitale* decision ruled that the State of New York, by encouraging the recitation of the Regents' prayer in its public school system, was in violation of the Establishment Clause in the First Amendment because "that prayer was composed by governmental

officials as a part of a governmental program to further religious beliefs."

2. Randy has authored three books on prayer and revival: *On Eagles' Wings* (Pacific Press®,1986), *If My People Pray* (Pacific Press®,1995), and *Bring Back the Glory* (Pacific Press®, 2000).

3. David Bryant, "Is This the Generation?" *Pray!* 8 (1998), 10.

4. "The Voluntary School Prayer Act of 1981," *Liberty*, November/December 1981, 6.

5. David Van Biema, "A Surge of Teen Spirit," *Time*, May 31, 1999, 58, 59.

6. Greg Brooks, "The Prayer Panacea," *Liberty*, May/June 1997, 20, 22.

7. Ibid., 20.

SPIRITUALITY

Our technological age is producing a surprising hunger for spirituality. It seems the deeper we venture into "cyberspace," the more we seek peace in the "inner space" of our souls. What does it mean to be a spiritual person today? Christians often substitute religious activity for spiritual growth with disastrous results.

I like this section because it addresses, among other things, the problem of dryness—that sad state that every Christian experiences at one time or another when Bible reading leaves us uninspired, prayers seem to hit the ceiling, and everything that used to bring us joy seems stale and lifeless. These eight chapters are bursting with ideas about how to restore your spiritual passion, ways to deal with guilt, how to know God's will for your life, and more. Share these chapters with a spouse or friend. Share them at prayer meeting or in your small group. Discuss them and put them to the test. I'm praying that these chapters will help you to rekindle your first love experience with God.

Ways to Be a More Spiritual Person

OK. Sooner or later it's coming. Another new year. Another clean slate. Stretching before you untarnished will lie a brand new gift of 12 months, 52 weeks, 365 days, 8,760 hours, 525,600 minutes, 31,536,000 seconds. And even if you decide to spare yourself the agony and guilt of making and breaking New Year's resolutions, this year you want to give more attention to spiritual things and get closer to God.

Great. But you know what? That desire you feel for God is not your idea, it's His. Think of it like a pager. You're going about your business—maybe in traffic or sitting in a meeting or on the golf course—when suddenly your hip begins vibrating. Or a series of beeps assaults your ears. It's your pager. Somebody wants you. If it's someone you want to talk to, you go to the nearest phone and call that person.

The desire for greater spirituality is God "beeping" you. He wants to get closer. And you don't have to wait until January 1 to respond to God's page. Your "new year" of spiritual growth can begin right now, today.

Let me suggest five things you can do to grow spiritually.

5 Steps to Christlike Living

1. ADMIT YOUR NEED.

This seems like an obvious step, but many people never get beyond the wishing stage because they won't admit they have a need.

Reread Jesus' rebuke to the Laodiceans in Revelation 3:14-18. The Laodiceans were neither hot nor cold spiritually. They were "lukewarm"—and nauseating to Christ. But His real frustration with these people was not their lukewarmness, it was their "I-don't-need-anything" attitude. Read it for yourself: "You say, 'I am rich; I have acquired wealth and do not need a thing.' But you do not realize that you are wretched, pitiful, poor, blind and naked."[1]

Lukewarmness is not a problem for God. He can rekindle the fires of first love in His children—*if* they will see themselves as they really are and admit their need.

How do you do this? In prayer, tell God how much you need Him. Give Him permission to show you your spiritual blind spots and to point out those areas in your life that need to be brought under His control. Keep a pad and pencil handy as you do this, and be ready to write down what God reveals to you. Go down the list and pray about each issue, admitting the truth about yourself and accepting God's forgiveness.

2. TAKE ACTION.

This step is directly related to the first. After admitting to God that we need help and giving Him permission to show us our faults, we must *do something!* Because mine is a sit-down job, because I'm nearing the end of my thirties, and because I don't use my recreation center membership as I should, I've developed a little "spare tire" around my middle. I admit I have a need all right, but the spare tire still isn't "flat." It isn't flat because I haven't taken myself to the gym and done something about it!

Bill Hybels, pastor of the famous Willow Creek Community Church, says, "The heart and soul of the Christian life is learning to hear God's voice and developing the courage to do what He tells us to do."[2] If you're going to grow spiritually, you're going to have to do what God tells you to do.

Start by making a plan. List your goals. Do you want to read the Bible every day? To memorize Scripture? To do some volunteer work in your community? Want more time for prayer? Write down your goals. Submit your list to the Lord. Then take action. Follow through.

3. STICK CLOSE TO CHRIST.

Jesus said, "Remain in me, and I will remain in you. No branch can bear fruit by itself; it must remain in the vine. Neither can you bear fruit unless you remain in me."[3] If you want to be a more spiritual person and more like Christ, you need to "remain in" or stick close to Him. You need time with Jesus.

Again Bill Hybels writes, "Any way you cut it, a key ingredient in authentic Christianity is *time*. Not leftover time, not throwaway time, but quality time. Time for contemplation, meditation, and reflection. Unhurried, uninterrupted time."[4]

Stop laughing and listen. I know what you're thinking: *Yeah, I need time with Jesus, but there's a problem—I don't have any time. I get up at 5:00 a.m., hit the ground running, and don't slow down until 11 or 12 at night. Having time with Jesus sounds poetic and nice, but in the real world— my world—it hardly ever happens.*

Realize this: Time with Jesus will never just "happen." You must plan for it, and you must be committed to it just as you're committed to going to work every day. It's that important.

Set a realistic goal. Start small—maybe just 15 minutes every day. What you do with that time is between you and God. You may sing, journal, enjoy times of silence, pray, read God's Word, etc. But start today, and make it first on your list.

4. GET A SPIRITUAL-ACCOUNTABILITY PARTNER.

Find someone who shares your desire to grow spiritually and ask that person to enter into partnership with you to achieve your respective spiritual goals. Your accountability partner may be your spouse or it may be a close friend or family member. The principle here is strength in numbers. "Two are better than one, because they have a good return for their work: If one falls down, his friend can help him up. But pity the man who falls and has no one to help him up."[5]

Simply put, we need help. An accountability partner will pray for and with you, and, as the name suggests, hold you accountable to the goals you've set for yourself. Ask the Lord to lead you to the right person to partner with. Ask that person to lunch. Share your goals over a meal and invite that person to be your accountability partner. This may be the most exciting and most important step in your spiritual growth plan.

5. GIVE YOURSELF AWAY.

The Dead Sea is literally "dead" because water flows in but doesn't flow out. It's a "selfish" body of water—only receiving and not giving. Christians can become like the Dead Sea when they constantly *take in* Bible study, church activities, sermons, seminars, etc., but seldom *give out* in the form of Christian witness or service to others.

If you really want to grow spiritually this year, look and pray for ways to give yourself away. Volunteer at the local hospital or homeless shelter. Rake your neighbor's leaves. Play golf with a friend or business associate who doesn't know Christ. Organize a painting party and freshen up a shut-in's kitchen or exterior trim. The point is this: Spirituality is more than just sitting around praying and reading. We grow most like Jesus when we're serving and ministering to others.

Well, there you have it. Five ways to be a more spiritual person. Not an exhaustive list by any means, but one to start with.

Now "grow in the grace and knowledge of our Lord and Savior Jesus Christ."[6]

Peace.

---

1. Verse 17.
2. Bill Hybels, *Too Busy Not to Pray* (Downers Grove, Illinois: InterVarsity Press, 1988), 99.
3. John 15:4.
4. Hybels, 100, emphasis supplied.
5. Ecclesiastes 4:9, 10.
6. 2 Peter 3:18.

Ways to Restore Your Spiritual Passion

I wrote a love note today to someone other than my wife. Now before you start to write me nasty letters, let me assure you that my wife would have given her complete approval. Let me explain.

I had a two-hour layover in Denver International Airport and decided to grab a bite to eat before my next flight. As I munched my salad and sandwich, I noticed writing on one of the wood chips that hid the soil in the planter where I sat. I picked the chip up and smiled. "Ramon was here," it said. As I returned the chip to the planter, I noticed that many others were also "tagged." Other travelers, too, had left behind brief scribblings for people like me to read.

The scribblings included sports slogans and messages to lovers. But my favorite had on one side the number 53 and a drawing of a baseball and bat and on the other the date and this message: "I ♥ Jesus. Rosalyn Galindo." Apparently Rosalyn is a proud ball player who is even prouder of her love for Jesus. She recorded her feelings on a small piece of wood in a food-counter planter where it could be found by another hungry traveler—someone who might

5 Steps to Christlike Living

even be hungry for something more satisfying than a Big Mac.

Love notes. Between lovers, they're expressions of passion. But with the passing of time, a couple kids, increased work demands, bloated schedules, a few extra pounds, and financial worries, sometimes the passion in a marriage gives way to boredom. Lovers who once fanned the flame of their desire with love notes and other expressions of devotion begin to take each other for granted and slowly drift apart.

What can happen in a marriage can also happen in a relationship with God. Not long ago I got a phone call from a friend of mine. She sounded tense, and when I asked how she was doing, she replied, "D-minus." I probed further. She said nothing in her life was going right. "I've gotten far away from God, and I can feel the results of my distance. I hate those I work with, I've fallen into destructive habits, and I've been crying my eyes out. I want to get close to God again."

I don't know where this article finds you today, but if you're feeling like a wanderer lost in a spiritual desert, God wants to take you to a better place. He wants to embrace you in His arms and restore your soul. He wants you to know that He's real and that He can give you renewed purpose and joy beyond measure.

Interested? The following tips are intended to give you a jump start toward restoring your spiritual passion.

1. DO AGAIN THE THINGS YOU DID AT FIRST.

When the church at Ephesus lost its first love, Jesus counseled them to "remember the height from which you have fallen! Repent and do the things you did at first."[1]

That counsel is still good today. Think back. What were the things you used to do when the whole experience of being saved by faith was fresh and new? Did you have early morning devotions? Did you participate in a small-group Bible study? Did you regularly find ways to share your faith with others? Chances are good that you look back on those "first-love" experiences fondly. If you want to recapture the spark in your walk with God, do again the things you did at first. And don't use your busy schedule as an excuse not to act. Being "too busy" leads us into the spiritual doldrums faster than anything else does.

2. REPENT.

Get out a sheet of paper and ask God to bring to your mind all the rivals that are presently stealing your affections, time, and energy from the Lord. My list would include things like late-night television, fatigue, and hit-and-miss Bible study. Other lists might include unhealthy relationships, substance abuse, teenagers in the home (I could list that one too!), or even one's job. Whatever the rivals are, list them and then confess them to God, asking Him to show you how to deal with each one. Don't be afraid to face your spiritual failures and call them by name.

3. PRAISE GOD.

Praise is the secret weapon God has given every child of His with which to defeat the enemy. I love what Paul Billheimer said: "Satan is allergic to praise, so where there is massive, triumphant praise, Satan is paralyzed, bound, and banished." If the passion has gone out of your relationship with God, recapture the fire by harnessing the power of praise. God dwells where His name is praised.[2] So if you're feeling lately that He has packed up and gone fishing, I suggest you take a praise break.

Need help getting started? Try praising God for His Name, His righteousness, His infinite creation, and His Word.[3] Take five minutes after reading this article and write down ten ways God has blessed you. Present your list to God in prayer, and get ready to experience a close encounter of the divine kind.

4. REMEMBER THE CROSS.

It is shocking but true: Many of us no longer find the sacrifice Jesus made on Calvary emotionally moving. We've come to regard the Cross with the same nonchalance we feel toward a bowl of oatmeal. Christians hear the story of Jesus' death so frequently that we tend to zone out and pursue more mentally challenging truths of doctrine or prophecy.

But it was at the cross that we fell in love with a God who loved us enough to die so that we might live. So, to regain the passion, prayer-

5 Steps to Christlike Living

fully relive the scenes of Jesus' final week by reading and meditating on Matthew 21–28; Mark 11–16; Luke 19–23; and John 12–21. As you read these passages, ask yourself *who, what, when, where,* and *why.* Write your answers in a notebook and watch the Holy Spirit bring home to you again the wonder of Calvary and of God's amazing grace.

5. RECLAIM YOUR PURPOSE.

Here's an important truth: If you don't know the purpose of a thing, you can only abuse it. If you don't know why you're a Christian, your relationship with Jesus Christ will suffer the abuse of neglect.

There's more to being a Christian than going to church once a week, singing hymns, giving offerings, and doing an occasional good deed. We're here to be Christ's ambassadors and witnesses, sharing the good news that we've been forgiven and that Jesus is coming soon.[4] Ask God to help you witness for Him again. You don't have to sell your possessions and head to the mission field. Simply offer to pray with someone, offer a "God bless you" to your mail carrier or grocery-store clerk, or write a letter of encouragement to someone who is lost in the same spiritual desert you've been wandering in.

Which brings me back to that love note I said I wrote. After reading Rosalyn's message, I grabbed a nice blank piece of wood from the lunch-counter planter. On one side of it I wrote: "Randy Maxwell, 6/22/98. I ♥ Jesus." On the flip-side I penned: "And Jesus loves you." It was my way of passing Rosalyn's torch—of passing on our mutual passion for Christ and His passion for each one of us to the next person who hungers for more than a sandwich.

Ain't love grand?

---

1. Revelation 2:5.
2. See Psalm 22:3.
3. See Psalms 115:1; 35:28; 150:2; and 56:10, respectively.
4. See 2 Corinthians 5:20; Acts 1:8.

Ways to Know God's Will for Your Life

The other day I was in a neighborhood drugstore, trying to kill time while my oldest daughter shopped for a friend's birthday present. My youngest promptly dragged me to the toy aisle to look at all the new Barbies. Naturally, I was thrilled to death to see Buckingham Palace Barbie and all her friends.

Just when the excitement was about to render me nauseous, I spotted it. There on the shelf, mixed in with miscellaneous doll accessories, was a toy I hadn't seen in years. It was spherical and completely black except for a small circle of white that framed the number 8. The sphere was filled with some type of liquid, and through a small window on its bottom, messages would appear as if by magic whenever the ball was vigorously shaken.

It was a Magic 8 Ball. Remember the fun you had as a kid "asking" the Magic 8 Ball questions, shaking it, and then peering into the tiny window waiting for your "answer"? Depending on your version of the ball, you probably got answers like, "Yes, definitely," "My sources say No," "Very doubtful," "Most likely," or "Really hazy." Remember how

41

5 Steps to Christlike Living

you felt when you asked the ball if that certain someone really liked you and you got a "Without a doubt" in the window? It was the modern equivalent to plucking petals off a daisy and ending up with "She loves me" on the last one.

Of course, it was just a game, and everyone knew it wasn't to be taken seriously. But seeing that Magic 8 Ball again reminded me of how many times I had wished for something like it that really worked when it comes to asking God questions about my life.

Discerning God's will is, for many, a most frustrating and perplexing exercise. I can recall the many times I walked beneath a canopy of stars on a clear summer night, poured my heart out to God, and wished with all my might that He would spell His answer out across the heavens in letters of fire.

You've been there, haven't you? Well, believe it or not, finding God's will doesn't have to be an Indiana Jones–type quest. In fact, Paul indicates that we can know the thoughts of God through the ministry of the Holy Spirit. "In the same way no one knows the thoughts of God except the Spirit of God. *We have not received the spirit of the world but the Spirit who is from God, that we may understand what God has freely given us. . . .* 'For who has known the mind of the Lord that he may instruct him?' *But we have the mind of Christ.*"[1]

Entire books have been devoted to this subject of knowing God's will. It is a very personal journey for each individual Christian. But allow me to offer five general principles that may help.

1. PRAY FOR GUIDANCE.

Begin at the beginning. Ask God to guide your choices. One of my favorite promises to claim when it comes to divine guidance is Proverbs 3:5: "Trust in the Lord with all your heart and lean not on your own understanding; in all your ways acknowledge him, and he will make your paths straight." Whether a big thing or small, in *all* your ways—in everything that concerns you—acknowledge or consult Him.

"But I do pray," I can hear you saying, "and all I get is silence. If anything, I get more confused and stressed as time passes without any indication of what I'm supposed to do." OK, I hear you. But don't overlook the first words in this promise: *"Trust in the Lord"*! Jesus told us that the Father knows what we need.[2] He's promised that if we consult Him first and give priority to His counsel on the subject, He will steer us in the right direction. Prayer is step one.

2. SPEND TIME IN GOD'S WORD.

God's will and His Word go together. When Jesus was tempted by Satan to rely on His own power to satisfy His need for food, He said: "Man does not live on bread alone, but on every word that comes from the mouth of God."[3] God's will is revealed in His Word. To understand God's plans, purposes, and ways, we must know His Word. In fact, there are some things we don't even need to pray about because God's Word clearly reveals His will on the subject.

I received an email message not long ago from a woman who wanted to know if she should continue living with a man who was reluctant to marry her. The woman was a Christian. Her live-in boyfriend was not. She also implied that their relationship was not platonic. My answer was not one she really wanted to hear, but God's views on sex outside of marriage and on spiritually unequal relationships are clear.[4]

When I wrote the woman back and gently presented the counsel of God's Word, she admitted that she knew all along what was right and said she was taking steps to end the relationship. Sometimes in our heart of hearts we know what we *ought* to do in certain situations, but we're hoping to find a loophole somewhere that will allow us to pursue what we *want* to do. A knowledge of God's Word will save us a lot of time and trouble as we seek to know His will.

3. GET COUNSEL.

Proverbs 11:14 (NKJV) says: "Where there is no counsel, the people fall; but in the multitude of counselors there is safety."[5] Put simply, get advice. After praying and consulting God's Word, part of the "listening" process involves getting unbiased input from those you respect and believe to be walking with the Lord.

5 Steps to Christlike Living

4. ANSWER THE "TEN QUESTIONS."

Some years ago a friend gave me the following list. I don't know who the author is, so I can't give him or her credit. But answering the following ten questions will improve your spiritual hearing as you listen for God's voice when making decisions.

1. What is my life agenda, my ultimate purpose? Is it to know and do the Lord's will?

2. Which of the alternatives before me will be congruent with this life agenda?

3. Can I do it and keep my priorities straight? Does it contradict any of my basic values?

4. Will it extend the kingdom of God in my own life and relationships and in society at large?

5. If I made that choice, would it glorify my Lord and help me to grow as a person?

6. Would the choice bring me into a deeper relationship with the Lord?

7. Does it enable the ultimate good of all concerned? (The word *ultimate* means that though the choice may initially cause pain or difficulty, in the end it will benefit everyone involved.)

8. Will this choice enhance or diminish my self-esteem? Will I be able to look back on it and still love and accept myself?

9. Will it cause stress, anxiety, or uneasiness of soul?

10. Can I take the Lord with me in every aspect of carrying out the decision?

5. ACT—IN FAITH.

Take action! Don't straddle the fence forever. Make a move, trusting God to direct your steps. I saw a billboard that said "It's easier to guide something that's already in motion."

Does God love you? Yes. Have you prayed and consulted Him in your decision? Yes. Have you consulted His Word, the counsel of friends, and weighed out the options honestly? Then take action and trust God to direct you. If, after all that, you did make a poor decision, can't God adjust your course and bring you back to where He wanted you to be? Of course! He's promised, and you can ask Him to do exactly that!

Realize, too, that God sometimes offers us more than one good option. You may not always be choosing between "right" and "wrong." God may present you with several good opportunities. Follow the counsel above, use the good sense He gave you, and choose, knowing that God's blessings aren't limited to only one path. If you walk humbly with Him, He can bless you in whichever choice you make.

Don't be afraid of failure. Fear only leaving God out of your plans. That's the only time we're truly left in the dark.

Go with God. He's better than any Magic 8 Ball—"Without a doubt"!

---

1. 1 Corinthians 2:11, 12, 16; emphasis supplied.
2. Matthew 6:32.
3. Matthew 4:4.
4. See 1 Thessalonians 4:3; 2 Corinthians 6:14, 15.
5. NKJV.

5
Ways to Grow Spiritually in the New Millennium

The fact that Jesus didn't come in the year 2000 may have been a mercy—at least for many American Christians. Before you write me off as a heretic, hear me out: It may have been a mercy because, according to recent polls, the faith of many is only superficial.

The Gallup Organization noted that while Easter Sunday services draw Americans back to church by the millions,[1] two in ten Protestant and Catholic adults don't understand the religious significance of the day.[2] "These findings," wrote Gallup, "point to a 'knowledge gap' in Americans' religious condition—the gap between Americans' state of faith and their lack of the most basic knowledge about that faith."[3] This is evidenced by one sorry statistic that shows that one in 10 Americans believe Noah's wife was Joan of Arc![4]

This spiritual superficiality is resulting in a "religion a la carte" mindset in which people pick and choose the items of belief they like. "Substantial proportions of traditional Christians, for example, subscribe to non-Christian beliefs and practices, such as reincarnation, channeling, astrology, and fortune telling."[5]

Back to my opening statement: The fact that Jesus didn't come in the year 2000 may have been a mercy. "The Lord is not slow in keeping His promise, as some understand slowness. He is patient with you, not wanting anyone to perish, but everyone to come to repentance."[6] Perhaps we should all stop to consider prayerfully how well we know Jesus, how prepared we are to meet Him, and how we can mature as His disciples in the new millennium.

1. MAKE SURE JESUS, NOT HYPE, IS THE SOURCE OF YOUR FAITH.

I hope you were ready for "Y2K" letdown. Preachers, politicians, talk-show hosts, and so-called "psychics" had been hyping the dawn of the new millennium for years. Christian bookstore shelves were lined with titles that screamed warnings about the "millennium bug" and the end of the world. The reality, of course, was that the big bad bug was no more troublesome than a flea—a minor irritant, not the end of civilization! The expectations of some for Jesus' return in glory reached unprecedented heights. How has the fact that the world did *not* end on January 1, 2000 affected your faith? Do you still believe? If hype and fear are the twin engines that drive your faith, disillusionment may tempt you to abandon your relationship with Christ like so many others through the centuries when their expectations went unrealized.

Keep Jesus at the center of your faith. Don't tie your zeal to the intensity of the latest natural disaster or military conflict. Doom sells, but it's not the right glue to cement a relationship with Christ.

2. STAY IN THE WORD.

Christians will need to cling to and know the Word of God even better in this century. Why? Because sound doctrine based on a "Thus saith the Lord" is going to be harder to come by. Paul warned Timothy: "The time will come when men will not put up with sound doctrine. Instead, to suit their own desires, they will gather around them a great number of teachers to say what their itching ears want to hear. They will turn their ears away from the truth and turn aside to myths."[7]

5 Steps to Christlike Living

We've seen the tragic results of putting one's faith in cults like Heaven's Gate. Paganism is once again on the rise, and as pressure mounts for people of faith to set aside doctrinal differences for the sake of unity, deals are being made with the devil and outright heresies are being winked at and tolerated. Jesus said, " 'Watch out that no one deceives you.' "[8] *Get back to the Bible!* It is the only weapon you have against the deceptions of the new age and the pseudo-Christianity now emerging on the scene.

After the crushing disappointment of His death, Jesus revived the broken spirits of two disciples, not with a miracle, but "beginning with Moses and all the Prophets, he explained to them what was said in all the Scriptures concerning himself."[9] Jesus wanted to establish the faith of His followers on His Word. If you haven't already done so, now is the time to establish a habit of feeding on the Word of God daily. Know what you believe and why. Remember, it's not good enough to have one Bible—or several—on your shelves. A recent Gatorade commercial asks "Is it in you?" The Word of God must be in you, not in your bookcase.

3. SLOW DOWN.

If you think life at the end of the twentieth century was fast, wait until you see what's coming in the twenty-first! Technology will continue to push us where we aren't ready to go. Computers will get faster and relationships will get shallower. That's why Christians must slow down! Without quiet reflection on the presence, grace, and word of God, we will never be "deep" in the things that really matter.

The revivalist Leonard Ravenhill said: "We want large bonuses for small investments in prayer. We want to sow radish seeds but reap a forest of redwoods."[10] Five minutes a day in the Word (if that much), a few scattered minutes in prayer (if we remember to pray), ninety minutes a week at church, and we want to have great experiences with God. But the crying need of the church today is not speed but *depth*.

Deepening our relationship with the Almighty in the new millennium will demand that we "be still and know that [He] is God."[11] Say "no" more often. Turn off the computer and the cell phone long enough to refresh your spirit. Give your cell phone, laptop, DVD player, TV, and VCR a day off, observe the Sabbath,[12] and allow your soul a chance to reconnect to the Creator without the interference of "the world." Time with God will cure us of spiritual shallowness.

4. BE READY TO MINISTER.

Paul wrote, "Let us not become weary in doing good, for at the proper time we will reap a harvest if we do not give up. Therefore, as we have opportunity, let us do good to all people, especially to those who belong to the family of believers."[13] In other words, keep working for Jesus. When Martin Luther was asked what he would do if he knew the world would end tomorrow, he replied, "I'd plant a tree today." Believers living in the twenty-first century ought to share that approach to the future.

There should be no question as to how we're to occupy the time until Jesus does, in fact, return. Don't bury your talents like the wicked servant in the parable.[14] Remember, "faith without works is *dead!*"[15] Get involved. Let Jesus catch you doing His will. Don't criticize the culture of this new millennium. Instead, be ready to minister. Remember, the gospel is relevant and valid in every age. No matter how we progress in terms of technology, we'll still need a Savior.

5. BE READY.

Keep your spiritual "bags" packed. Jesus told the story of the ten virgins to His disciples so that they would know how to wait for His return. Five of the virgins took extra oil for their lamps; the other five did not. There was a delay. While the bridegroom tarried, the women fell asleep. At midnight, when the bridegroom approached, the virgins readied their lamps, which by now were burning low and about to go out. The five who brought oil filled their lamps and joined the bridal party. The five who failed to bring oil were left outside, unprepared and unrecognized. " 'Therefore keep watch,' " Jesus said about His coming, " 'because you do not know the day or the hour.' "[16]

The oil in the parable represents the Holy Spirit, who alone can drive home the truths of Scripture to our hearts. We obtain the "oil" every day as we abide in Christ, stay in His Word, slow down and get deeper, do the works of righteousness, and allow the Holy Spirit to change us from the inside out.

Jesus may come this year, or He may come years from now. Whenever He does come, let Him find us hard at work, leading others to the Light.

---

1. "Easter Draws Americans Back to Church," by George Gallup Jr., *Poll Releases*, April 2, 1999: Internet: <http://www.gallup.com/poll/releases/pr990402b.asp>.

2. Ibid.

3. Ibid.

4. "Barna's poll numbers," taken from George Barna's latest book, *The Index of Leading Spiritual Indicators*, which offers a statistical report on the state of religion in America. Internet: <http://www.smythnews.com/970118/I-Articles/re-2.htm)>.

5. "Easter Draws Americans Back to Church," by George Gallup Jr., *Poll Releases*, April 2, 1999: Internet: <http://www.gallup.com/poll/releases/pr990402b.asp>.

6. 2 Peter 3:9.

7. 2 Timothy 4:3, 4.

8. Matthew 24:4.

9. Luke 24:27.

10. Psalm 46:10.

11. Leonard Ravenhill, *Revival Praying* (Minneapolis: Bethany House Publishers, 1996), 141.

12. See Exodus 20:8-11; Hebrews 4:9, 10.

13. Galatians 6:9, 10.

14. See Matthew 25:14-30.

15. James 2:17, emphasis added.

16. Matthew 25:13.

Ways to Be Free in Jesus

Remember the hijacking of that TWA flight back in the 1980s? I remember it because of the amazing press conference arranged by the terrorists for the hostages. Those hostages, including the pilots of the aircraft, were seen by millions on TV. Everyone wanted to know how they were faring, how their Shiite Muslim captors were treating them. The hostages' facial expressions stood out in my mind as I watched; their faces contradicted what was coming from their mouths. Their lips were saying things like "We're well. We're receiving fine treatment." But they didn't *look* "well." Their faces bore deep lines of anxiety, stress, and trauma. And this was to be expected, because regardless of how well they were allegedly being treated, they were *still* hostages, *still* captives under the gun. *Still not free!*

Imagine with me a slightly different scenario. What would viewers conclude if TV cameras were allowed to roll in our churches? What would people see on their TV screens if the press descended upon our sanctuaries and put the question to us: "You're Christians. Tell us, how do you feel? Are you being cared for? What message would you

5 Steps to Christlike Living

like to send to your family, friends, and the people of the world?"

I'm sure the viewers would hear many wonderful testimonies. But I wonder if they would come to the same conclusion most of us did as we watched the hostages—that however comforting and uplifting the words coming from our lips might be, our faces revealed that all is not well. That we, while claiming to be free in Jesus, claiming to be the happiest people on earth, are still bound, still in captivity, still held hostage, still not free!

The term *joyless Christian* should be an oxymoron. Yet, there are whole congregations that are as devoid of joy as a tomb is devoid of life. Why is this?

I received the following heartbreaking letter:

> I'm 46 years old, and it seems the older I get, the more confused and disillusioned I am. [In my denomination] I was never taught to praise God in any way, shape, or fashion. I agree with what you say, but I have this notion ingrained in my being that any sort of praise, other than to quietly say "Amen," [is not acceptable]. Our religion is based on doctrine, not praise, not emotion, . . . not sharing! We've missed the boat in my opinion. We are more concerned about issues and things (appearances and being right) than what Jesus has done for us in our daily lives. . . . I'm so frustrated I could scream.

If you identify with this writer's feelings of bondage, consider the following suggestions for being free in Jesus.

1. ENCOURAGE YOURSELF IN THE LORD.

First Samuel 30 recounts the story of David at Ziklag. The Amalekites had taken advantage of David's absence and had sacked the city while it was left unguarded. They kidnapped his wives and the wives and children of his soldiers and burned their homes to the ground. Verse 4 records that "David and his men wept aloud until they had no strength left to weep." After the tears, things got worse for David—his men became enraged and threatened to stone him.

What was David's response to the blackness and despair swirling about him? "David *encouraged himself* in the Lord His God."[1]

> In this hour of utmost extremity David, instead of permitting his mind to dwell upon these painful circumstances, looked earnestly to God for help. He "encouraged himself in the Lord." He reviewed his past eventful life. Wherein had the Lord ever forsaken him? His soul was refreshed in recalling the many evidences of God's favor[2]

The word *encouraged* in verse six means "strengthened" or seized hold of. If you truly want to be free from depression and forbidding circumstances, seize hold of the Lord your God. Fortify your mind against the harassments of the enemy and, like David, refresh your soul by recalling the many evidences you have of God's favor. Don't count on some preacher, choir, worship symposium, or magazine to lift you from the spiritual doldrums. Encourage yourself in the Lord.

2. LAUGH AGAIN.

Remember the little girl who asked her mom if cows were Christians? Mom responded, "No! Why would you think a thing like that?" "Well," the little girl explained, "they all have such long faces."[3]

Cultivate a wholesome sense of humor. Laugh again! Laugh at yourself, and laugh with others. Get a Mark Lowry video. (If you can keep a straight face through this Christian comedian's routine, you're dead!) And do yourself one more favor: Get your hands on the Visual Bible video presentation of *The Gospel According to Matthew*, starring Bruce Marchiano in the role of Jesus.[4] Using only the words of the New International Version of the book of Matthew, Marchiano brings to the screen a unique vision of Jesus as you've never seen Him—a *joyful* Jesus! A Jesus who *smiles!* A Jesus who *laughs* and whose face shouts YES!

Some Christians like their Jesus somber and serious. They like to focus on the "Man of sorrows" aspect of His mission. I prefer Luke's description of Jesus as being "full of joy through the Holy Spirit."[5] Doesn't it make you feel good inside when you think of Jesus' face breaking into a wide smile whenever He hears or speaks your name?

3. SING TO THE LORD.

Where on earth did we Christians get the idea that God wants our worship to be solemn, long-faced, and quiet? David said: "I will be glad and rejoice in you; I will sing praise to your name, O Most High." "Shout for joy to the Lord, all the earth, burst into jubilant song with music; make music to the Lord with the harp, with the harp and the sound of singing."[6]

The Hebrew word translated "rejoice" in Psalm 9:2 is *alats*. It means "jump for joy"! I understand reverence and the need for an appreciation of God's awesome holiness. Apparently, however, emotions of joy that produce the responses of "jubilant song," "shouting," and even "jumping for joy" aren't contrary to the worship of a holy God. I'm not advocating bedlam, but please, in our worship services, make room for the joyful expressions of praise! If we don't, we're not giving a complete picture of God. Sing with enthusiasm in church, and bring song into your prayer closet. Sing to the Lord and see the shackles of gloom and despondency dissolve.

4. WITNESS AGAIN.

"My lips will shout for joy when I sing praise to you—I, whom you have redeemed. My tongue will tell of your righteous acts all day long."[7] Remember witnessing? It saddens me to think that for many of us, sharing our faith is becoming a dim memory. Nothing sets the soul free like sharing our freedom in Christ with someone else. What has God done for you? Through email, "snail mail," by phone, or in person, open your mouth and bear witness to God's "righteous acts" in your life. There is absolutely nothing in this world that will lift you spiritually and fill you with joy faster than seeing another person come to Jesus because of your testimony.

5. POSSESS YOUR POSSESSIONS.

If you don't know who you are in Christ or what His blood entitles you to, read Ephesians 1. The list of your "possessions" includes "every spiritual blessing in Christ," being "chosen . . . to be holy and blameless," "adoption," "redemption through His blood," "the forgiveness of sins," knowing the "mystery of His will," "inclusion" in Christ, and "the promised Holy Spirit, who is a deposit guaranteeing our inheritance until the redemption of *those who are God's possession.*"[8]

Did you notice that last phrase? You are God's possession! You belong to Him and you have every right to rejoice (to "jump for joy"), to enjoy the freedom Jesus brings. Don't let circumstances, Satan, or even sober saints steal your joy and force you to eat spiritual cheese and crackers when you've been invited to feast at the Savior's banquet table. You are not a hostage. Claim your freedom. In Jesus, be free. And "if the Son sets you free, you will be free indeed."[9]

---

1. Verse 6, KJV.

2. Ellen G. White, *Patriarchs and Prophets* (Nampa, Idaho: Pacific Press®, 1958), 692.

3. Ginny Allen told this story in "The Joy Response," *ParentTalk*, November/December 1996, 31.

4. You can obtain the three-volume series The Visual Bible from your local Christian bookstore or by calling 1-800-780-VIDEO.

5. Luke 10:21.

6. Psalms 9:2; 98:4, 5.

7. Psalm 71:23, 24.

8. Emphasis supplied.

9. John 8:36.

Ways to Increase Your Faith

When I was writing these articles for *Signs of the Times*®, I received dozens of letters and emails each month. I tried to answer each one, but often the volume of mail overwhelmed me and I could only get to a few. This particular email, however, caught my attention. I thought many of the readers of this book would identify with it.

> I constantly struggle with faith. I pray and seek God's will and trust God will make a way. However, at times I find myself not remaining quite so solid. I know that God is near and hears my prayers, but somehow I get so lost. Would you please discuss having faith and believing that God will answer your prayers when you pray? I understand the importance of believing, but when you believe, what's the next step?

Faith. It's the bedrock of Christianity. Yet for many of us, explaining faith is like trying to nail Jell-O to the wall. Snake handlers believe Mark 16:18 tells them that faith will protect them from the serpent's deadly venom. Thousands flock to see statues of the Virgin Mary shed bloody tears, believing that they will be healed if their faith is strong enough. Many others believe in "faith confession" in which you "name it and claim it" and get rich, hitched, or healed based on what you say about the promises in God's Word. Still others rely on supernatural manifestations or ecstatic experiences—such as being "slain in the Spirit"—as proof that their faith is strong.

What is true faith, and how much of it must we have in order to please God? What do you do after you've believed and prayed?

1. TRUST IN WHO GOD IS MORE THAN IN WHAT YOUR FAITH CAN DO.

Another word for *faith* is *trust*. When faith is genuine, it trusts God in all circumstances—even when our prayers aren't answered the way we thought they would be. Pay close attention to the examples of faith recorded in Hebrews 11. Sure, you have your Josephs and Moseses and Gideons—those who through faith "conquered kingdoms, . . . shut the mouths of lions, quenched the fury of the flames, and escaped the edge of the sword." But mentioned right alongside these heroes are others who "were tortured," "stoned," "sawed in two." Who "wandered in deserts and mountains, and in caves and holes in the ground."

Hebrews says, "These were all commended for their faith, yet none of them received what had been promised."[1]

Why did some of God's friends "gain what was promised" while others did not? Was it because of a lack of faith? Absolutely not! The Bible says they were *all* "commended for their faith." Faith isn't something you strain to work up. And hard times or a No answer to prayer doesn't necessarily indicate a lack of faith. The faith described in Hebrews 11 is an unbending trust in who God is. It's a relationship with God that teaches you to trust Him in all circumstances—even when things don't work out as planned. Just ask the "others" in God's faith hall of fame.

2. KEEP PRAYING.

Jesus told His disciples a parable about a widow who kept asking a judge for justice.[2] For a while, the judge refused to grant her plea, but the woman wouldn't go away. Through relentless pressure, she wore him down. In time, the judge said, " ' "Even though I don't fear God or care about men, yet because this widow keeps bothering me, I will see that she gets justice, so that she won't eventually wear me out with her coming!" ' " Jesus' point was that if a wicked judge will grant justice to a persistent petitioner, how much more will a loving God " 'bring about justice for his chosen ones, who cry out to him day and night?' "

After making this point, He asked the following question: " 'However, when the Son of Man comes, will he find faith on the earth?' " The context of this parable indicates that Jesus was asking if, when He returns, *He will find those who will pray and not give up.*

Faith is holding on to God and not letting go! Adopt the acronym P.U.S.H.: Pray Until Something Happens! There are times when Satan attempts to intercept the blessings we seek.[3] Other times, our request is on target but our timing is off. And yet other times, the Lord tests our desire and resolve. The point is that we are to "pray and not give up." This is the kind of faith Jesus will be looking for when He comes again.

3. OBEY (ACT) DESPITE YOUR DOUBTS.

Another definition of faith is obeying despite your doubts. Even if your knees are knocking and your teeth are chattering, what we *do* is always more important than what we *feel* inside. Look again at Hebrews 11. "By faith the people passed through the Red Sea as on dry land."[4] Do you think those newly freed slaves walked with confidence through the walls of water? I think they ran for their lives, terrified that the sea might collapse on them and terrified that Pharaoh's army might catch up with them. But, scared or not, they *went through!* They obeyed the command God gave through Moses. They acted, and that act of obedience is commended as "faith" in Hebrews 11.

Ever been afraid of following what you believe to be God's will? When I moved my wife and daughter from Los Angeles to Nampa, Idaho, I was scared to death! I didn't feel *brave* or *confident* or any other of those super-faithful feelings you imagine you're supposed to have when you're trusting God. But I believed the move to be God's will. He had supplied the evidence of His leading. And so, with much fear and trembling, I obeyed. I took action. God says that's faith!

If you don't have super-spiritual *feelings* of confidence, just pray the prayer of the father whose son had an evil spirit: " 'I do believe; help me overcome my unbelief!' "[5]

4. BELIEVE THAT YOU RECEIVE.

Mark 11:24 records Jesus' instruction: " 'Whatever you ask for in prayer, believe that you have received it, and it will be yours.' "

How do you do this? Thank God for the answer even before you receive it. But before you start thanking Him for winning the Power Ball jackpot or receiving that $70,000 automobile, remember that our prayers need to be consistent with His will. (Isn't it interesting how often we interpret Jesus' promises to mean we can have fancy *material* things when Jesus' whole life was one of simplicity, humility, and service?) The apostle James explained, "When you ask, you do not receive, *because you ask with wrong motives, that you may spend what you get on your pleasures.*"[6] Apparently, it is possible to pray with incorrect motives—to ask for things outside of God's will.

But the Bible is full of things we can pray for with assurance that they are within God's will for us. These would include forgiveness, adoption, eternal life, reconciliation, the new birth, peace with God, and the Holy Spirit. "We need look for no outward evidence of the blessing. The gift is in the promise, and we may go about our work assured that what God has promised He is able to perform, and that the gift, *which we already possess*, will be realized when we need it most."[7]

5. "WEIGHT" ON THE LORD.

No, I'm not simply trying to be cute or clever. I believe that when the Lord tells us to "wait," He has more in mind than our sitting in a corner with our Bibles, wringing our hands. I believe God wants us to w-e-i-g-h-t on Him—to place the full weight of our burden, whatever it is, totally on Him and thereby receive a fresh supply of strength to carry on.[8] Isn't that what the apostle Peter means by these words: "Cast all your anxiety on him because he cares for you"?[9]

5 Steps to Christlike Living

If we truly let go of our troubles when we give them to God, He will renew our strength,[10] and we, in turn, will learn to trust Him more. And that's the bottom line to faith.

---

1. Hebrews 11:33-39.

2. See Luke 18:1-8.

3. See Daniel 10:1-14.

4. Hebrews 11:29.

5. Mark 9:24.

6. James 4:3; emphasis supplied.

7. Ellen G. White, *Education* (Nampa, Id.: Pacific Press®, 1952), 258; emphasis supplied.

8. Read more about this concept of waiting on God in my book *On Eagles' Wings*, (Pacific Press®, 1997), ISBN 0-8163-13458. You may order this book by calling 1-800-765-6955, or read a sample chapter and order online at: <http://www.adventistbookcenter.com>.

9. 1 Peter 5:7.

10. See Isaiah 40:31.

5 Ways to Deal With Guilt

I don't know why I lied. There was no reason. I just did. And almost a full year later my conscience was still beating me up. The guilt felt like a noose around my neck.

It started at summer camp. I was 12 years old and just finishing a week away from home in the San Bernardino mountains. The week had been great, filled with all the typical delights of summer camp: hiking, boating, horseback riding, campfire stories, raids on the girls' cabins (just heard about them, didn't participate), model-car building, etc. On the bus headed for home, I discovered I was a dollar short on the money my parents had given me to spend at camp. I knew they'd ask me if I had spent it all, so I looked everywhere for that dollar. Alas! it was nowhere to be found.

Sure enough, after a hug-filled reunion with my folks, my mom asked whether I had spent all the money they had given me. I panicked. I didn't want to confess that I had lost it. Fear of punishment blurred my judgment, and before I knew what I was doing I heard the word Yes coming from my mouth.

5 Steps to Christlike Living

I lied to my mother! However bad it was to lose money, I had just compounded the crime by lying about it. In my family, lying was the ultimate crime. You might get by with other sins, but you *never* lied!

Well, the days turned into weeks, the weeks turned into months, and the guilt got heavier and heavier. Though my parents were blissfully unaware of my deceit and my life appeared to roll on normally, my secret sin was stealing my joy, consuming my thoughts, and erecting an invisible barrier in our relationship.

Guilt. How do we deal with it? We've all felt it, and some of us never get rid of it. It can be brought on by something as small as lying about lost spending money or by something as big as an adulterous affair. People who are riddled with guilt cannot function normally. They may withdraw into a shell of self-loathing, feeling that they deserve all the bad things in life that come their way. Or they may lash out in anger or develop an addiction to drugs, sex, or gambling to mask the pain of a guilty conscience.

For Christians, guilt is often a greater puzzle. Feelings of guilt often make it impossible for us to grasp the concept of forgiveness and God's unconditional love. Guilt tells us we're beyond hope, lost, and that God could never love anyone as detestable as we are. Christians in this condition may attend church faithfully, sing in the choir, and work harder than others in the congregation. But inside they feel no joy, no assurance of salvation—only the gnawing fear that ultimately, when they stand before the judgment seat of Christ, they will hear the words, "Depart from me, I never knew you."

Let me suggest five ways to deal with unresolved guilt.

1. DISTINGUISH BETWEEN TRUE AND FALSE GUILT.

Both the Lord and the devil use guilt. That's right. The difference is in *how* they use it.

When God uses guilt, it's for the purpose of *conviction*—to persuade us of the wrongness of our actions so we will come to Him for forgiveness and cleansing. The Holy Spirit is the One who does this work of conviction. Describing the Spirit's role, Jesus said, " 'When he comes, he will convict the world of guilt in regard to sin and righteousness and judgment.' "[1]

At first, this may sound negative. But remember, the Holy Spirit is also called the Comforter. He doesn't expose our guilt to drive us to despair. Rather, " 'he will guide you into all truth.' "[2] He helps to move us to where we can see our need of God—the God who " 'did not send his Son into the world to condemn the world, but to *save* the world through him.' "[3]

Satan, on the other hand, uses guilt as a sledgehammer of *condemnation*. He is "the accuser of our brothers, who accuses them before our God day and night."[4] He intends to make us feel cut off from Christ and to convince us that we don't deserve forgiveness.

Here's how to tell if you're experiencing true or false guilt. If you actually have done something wrong and you're feeling that your relationship with God has suffered a blow and you want to restore that relationship as quickly as possible, that's the Holy Spirit convicting you—showing you the truth.

If, on the other hand, you are feeling too unworthy to come to Christ and that you may as well give up, that's the Accuser using false guilt to bring condemnation.

Christ brings conviction; Satan brings condemnation.

2. MAKE IT RIGHT WITH GOD.

David knew that his sin with Bathsheba was first of all a sin against God. He prayed, "Against you, you only, have I sinned and done what is evil in your sight."[5] He made no attempt to sugarcoat what he'd done. He confessed the sin and asked God for mercy, forgiveness, and cleansing.

The surest way to deal with guilt is to go to God and honestly confess what you have done. We have God's word that "if we confess our sins, He is faithful and just to forgive us our sins and to cleanse us from all unrighteousness."[6]

3. MAKE IT RIGHT WITH THE OFFENDED PARTY.

If your sin is against another person, the next step is to seek forgiveness from that person. According to Jesus, making things right with an offended brother or sister is even more important than worship![7]

5 Steps to Christlike Living

I remember one day when I was in a foul mood and snapped at my wife. The moment I did, I knew I was wrong and needed to apologize. *But it was so hard to admit that I had been acting like a jerk!* My pride was taking a beating (a good thing!), and I wrestled with my guilt. Finally, I went to my bride and confessed that I had been a jerk (no news to her!) and that I was sorry for snapping at her. "Please forgive me," I said, feeling very ashamed and very exposed. Instantly, the tension between us dissolved, and she eagerly accepted my apology. Our relationship was restored, and my guilt evaporated.

When you hurt someone, confess it and make a sincere apology as quickly as possible. Don't let resentments fester unresolved. "Do not let the sun go down while you are still angry"[8] continues to be good advice.

4. IF POSSIBLE, MAKE RESTITUTION.

If you can repair the damages your actions have caused, do it. Restitution may mean making good on missed alimony payments or replacing items that you've lost, damaged, or stolen.

Damaged emotions, however, are harder to deal with. How, for instance, do you make restitution for the emotional wounds you may have inflicted on a child or spouse by psychological or physical abuse? Only God can heal the resulting scars on the soul. After making things right with God and the person or persons you've hurt, seeking professional help may be the next best thing to making restitution.

5. REPENT, RELEASE, AND REJOICE.

Repentance is more than just feeling sorry that you've sinned. It is the deliberate choice to change your actions. Literally, it means to "turn around" and go in another direction. The Bible says, "He who has been stealing must steal no longer."[9] This is true repentance—sorrow followed by a change of mind, heart, and actions.

Once the sin has been confessed and repented of, release both it and the guilt that goes with it. God says that He casts our sins into the depths of the sea.[10] Then, don't go deep sea diving looking for them! Accept God's forgiveness and don't look back. When we cling to the guilt of sins long ago confessed, forsaken, and repented of, we're believing Satan, "the father of lies," and doubting God, who cannot lie.[11]

Finally, rejoice that you are forgiven! "Blessed is he whose transgressions are forgiven, whose sins are covered."[12]

Speaking of rejoicing, I finally confessed to my mom that I lied about the missing spending money. No punishment could be worse than the daily torment my guilt was giving me.

Know what happened? My mom hugged me close and told me how happy she was that I told the truth. Forgiveness! Instant relief. Goodbye to guilt.

Amazing grace, how sweet the sound!

---

1. John 16:8.
2. Verse 13.
3. John 3:17.
4. Revelation 12:10.
5. Psalm 51:4.
6. 1 John 1:9.
7. See Matthew 5:23, 24.
8. Ephesians 4:26.
9. Ephesians 4:28.
10. See Micah 7:19.
11. See John 8:44; Numbers 23:19; Hebrews 6:18.
12. Psalm 32:1.

Ways to Overcome the Spiritual Blahs

This chapter first appeared in an October issue of *Signs*, but I wrote it in early January. Idahoans had suffered through more than a week of gray, sunless skies and freezing temperatures. It was bleak, monotonous, and gloomy. The southern Idaho landscape where I live is rather blah in winter, and when high pressure builds over us, the Treasure Valley gets socked in with an oppressive inversion of smoke and fog that acts like a lid on a pot, hiding the sun for days, even weeks on end.

Ever have a spiritual inversion settle over your walk with the Lord? You know what I'm talking about. Those gray days when you feel like the Christian race you're running has become a monotonous trudge through the fog. Nothing seems right. You read your Bible just the way you've always done, but for some reason the words don't seem to say anything to you and you find no comfort in them. Your prayer life becomes an empty habit—lifeless, tedious, and a drudgery. Christian virtues like love, longsuffering, purity, and commitment seem dull and unattractive. Your conscience becomes insensitive and blunt, and the still, small voice is squelched to a hoarse whisper. Such period of spiritual dryness can cause a tremendous amount of internal turmoil. You'll likely torture yourself with the question, Why can't I love God the way I should? Why can't I love Him like I have in the past?[1]

I have felt this way many times. The spiritual blahs are frustrating and perplexing because many times they strike when things are relatively calm. How do you break through the spiritual doldrums and get "fired up" again?

1. PERSEVERE.

When asked by a friar what he should do when he felt dry and empty during prayer, Brother Giles of Assisi replied: "Labor faithfully and devoutly, because the grace that God does not give you at one time He may give you at another time. And what He does not give you one day or one week or month or year, He could give you another day or another week or month or year. Place your labor firmly in God, and God will place His grace in you as it may please Him. A metal worker making a knife strikes many blows on the iron out of which he is making the knife before the knife is finished. But finally the knife is finished with one blow."[2]

Feelings come and feelings go. Fatigue, stress, hormones, the weather, diet—all affect our moods. Feeling dry or spiritually blah does not mean God has forsaken us or that we've somehow lost our salvation. Fix the factors—such as rest and diet—that you can, then keep coming to God in prayer. This is an act of faith, and believers walk by faith and not by sight (or feelings). The feelings will come. In the meantime, stay close to God.

2. READ YOUR PRAYER JOURNAL.

If you keep prayer journals in which you write out prayers to God, get some of your old ones and reread them. I have found this exercise to be a most effective "boredom buster." Even when my Bible reading leaves me flat and uninspired, when I read through the pages of my prayer journal where I've poured out my heart to God, I'm often encouraged by the recollection of how God intervened on my behalf. I see with my own eyes that God has a track record with me—

that my prayers don't bounce off the ceiling; that He really *has* been active in my life, calming my fears and guiding me through tough situations.

If you don't keep a prayer journal, let me encourage you to do so. Simply write your prayers in the form of letters to God. Date them, and keep your entries in a notebook of some kind. These prayers and notations as to their answers become a written record of your spiritual journey with God. Reading these "conversations" you've had with the Lord will lift you above the "fog."

3. ADOPT THE LORD'S FAST.

When we think of fasting, we primarily think of abstaining from food, but the prophet Isaiah introduces us to another fast that pleases the Lord even more:

> "Is not this the kind of fasting I have chosen: to loose the chains of injustice and untie the cords of the yoke, to set the oppressed free and break every yoke? Is it not to share your food with the hungry and to provide the poor wanderer with shelter—when you see the naked, to clothe him, and not turn away from your own flesh and blood?"[3]

This is the Lord's fast. It is a fast from selfishness. A fast from thinking about your own ease and comfort. Spiritual dryness may be the result of failure to "feed" others. You can't constantly take in God's Word through preaching, teaching, etc., and not expect to get spiritually overweight and sluggish if you don't share some of that good stuff with others. So, share what you have, be joyful in giving, and stop looking at your faults and shortcomings. Get involved with helping someone else and . . .

"Then your light will break forth like the dawn, and your healing will quickly appear. . . . Then you will call, and the Lord will answer; you will cry for help, and he will say: Here am I. . . . The Lord will guide you always; he will satisfy your needs in a sun-scorched land and will strengthen your frame. You will be like a well-watered garden, like a spring whose waters never fail."[4]

4. CONFESS CHERISHED SIN.

Another source of the spiritual blahs is cherished sin. By this I mean clinging to something that you know to be outside the will of God.

Let me make it plain. It's hard to feel spiritually close to God when you're cheating on your spouse! That's an extreme example, I know, but the point is that sin is a barrier to our walk with God.

> Surely the arm of the Lord is not too short to save, nor his ear too dull to hear. *But your iniquities have separated you from your God; your sins have hidden his face from you, so that he will not hear.*[5]

Confess your sin to God, accept His forgiveness and His power to help you live within His will.[6] Living a life consistent with God's will as revealed in His Word is a sure cure for the spiritual blahs.

5. GET SOME REST.

Back in chapter 3 I mentioned this same item, but it bears repeating. We're not getting enough sleep. Forty percent of adults say that they are so sleepy during the day that it interferes with their daily activities.[7] (You're probably one of them!)

We're on the go from the time our feet hit the floor in the morning until the time our heads hit the pillow at night. We're like gerbils on an exercise wheel—running fast but going nowhere! When we finally do sit still, we immediately fall asleep. When you're that tired, it's nearly impossible to have a productive "quiet time" in prayer and in God's Word.

Pay attention to the amount of rest you're getting each night. Stick to a regular schedule for going to bed and waking up, even on weekends. Give yourself permission to lie down and get some rest. That's right—go ahead, take a nap. Schedule it. Set your alarm and go for that much needed sleep. Only promise yourself that you will awaken, not to the next item on your To Do list, but to a period of silence and solitude with the Lord.

Know what happened today? The sun came out. It was brief, but I saw it, and it lifted my spirits just to know it was still there. The clouds and grayness of winter don't last forever, and neither do the spiritual blahs. Though you may not "feel" Him, the Son is near. Try these simple suggestions and trust God to warm your heart once again.

---

1. "The Spiritual Doldrums," radio script by Shirley Maxwell for *Perfect Peace Ministries*, © 1983.

2. From *The Little Flowers of St. Francis*, by St. Francis of Assisi, as quoted in "Persevering Through Dry Seasons in Prayer," *Discipleship Journal*, No. 88 (1995), 94.

3. Isaiah 58:6, 7.

4. Verses 8, 9, 11.

5. Isaiah 59:1, 2, emphasis supplied.

6. See 1 John 1:9; Philippians 2:13.

7. "How Sleepy Are You? 1999 U.S. Sleep Survey Shows Disturbing Trends in Daytime Sleepiness," <www.sleepfoundation.org/PressArchives/lead.html>.

RELATIONSHIPS

Relationships are what Christlike living is all about. What goes on in our homes reveals the authenticity of our relationship with God. In these four chapters you will find some practical advice for how to improve your marriage and your relationship with your children. Of special interest will be the two chapters discussing spiritually divided marriages. If you're married to someone who doesn't share your convictions, you'll want to check these out.

Ways to Romance Your Spouse

Do you have any idea what one night of romance in a hotel without the kids can do for your marriage? A *lot*, believe me! As an anniversary present, my parents, in cahoots with our three daughters, gave Suzette and me a child-free night in a brand-new hotel built to aid couples in finding the romance in their marriages again.

The gift couldn't have been more appreciated or come at a better time. The three months leading up to our nineteenth anniversary had been extremely stressful. Work demands, school schedules, basketball games, gymnastic practices, term papers, final exams, prayer conferences, choir programs, and piano recitals had converged in unprecedented fury, and our emotional energy reserves were about as low as they could be. During this time, romance took a back seat to survival. Most nights it was a race to see who would start snoring first.

The routine was beating us down, and fatigue was sapping all the zest and sizzle right out of our relationship. Then we had our night at the Anniversary Inn. Instead of hustling kids into the van to get somewhere on time, barking out table-manner commands like a drill ser-

73

geant, fixing lunches, getting little ones showered down and dressed for bed, picking Cheerios out of the sofa cushions, etc., there was soft music, candlelight, bubble bath, and scented oils. And best of all, there were *no children!* (I really do love my kids!)

The transformation was dramatic. In an atmosphere of total relaxation and pampering, we discovered that the old "magic" was still there. That we could still have a coherent conversation, and that we were still human beings. We had allowed children, stress, jammed schedules, and fatigue torob us of something precious—our couplehood.

In a book on bringing romance back into our lives, Ed Young noted that a recent L.A. *Times* poll of two thousand adults revealed that the overwhelming majority, when asked about their main goal in life, responded, "to be happily married."[1] Yet so many marriages are in trouble. What has gone wrong?

Surely one big problem is the lack of romance in our relationships. Years, children, and the pace of life hammer away at a marriage, and we look up one day and discover that the words of that old Righteous Brothers hit, "You've Lost That Lovin' Feeling," apply to us.

So what's the answer? With the Anniversary Inn fading from view in our rearview mirror and knowing I had to write this article, I turned to Suzette and asked her what she found romantic. I've combined her advice with some gems I gathered from other guests at the Anniversary Inn who had shared nuggets of wisdom in journals located in each room.

1. NEVER STOP TRYING TO SPOIL EACH OTHER.

To put a spiritual slant on this, try to "out serve" each other. The Bible says, "Each of you should look not only to your own interests, but also to the interests of others."[2] This works for marriages too. Make a conscious effort to put your spouse's needs first. Go on a campaign to see how much you can "spoil" your mate. Rub her feet at the end of the day. Fix his favorite meal. Take the kids to the park for a few hours so she will have some time to herself. Watch Monday night football with him. Go wild. Be creative.

And while you're at it, keep Hebrews 10:24 in mind: "In response to all he [Christ] has done for us, let us outdo each other in being helpful and kind to each other and in doing good."[3] A mutual "spoiling" contest will definitely put the spark back in your relationship.

2. WRITE NOTES OF SUPPORT AND AFFECTION.

This is one of my wife's favorites. Write love notes and Scriptures that have special meaning to your spouse. Leave these little "care packages" on the bathroom mirror or in her purse or car. Once I left a little "I love you" note on the driver's seat of my car when I parked at the airport. I knew Suzette would be coming later to pick up the car and would see the note when she got in. I got a lot of pleasure out of imagining the smile on her face when she saw that little message.

Notes of encouragement, expressions of thanks and support, are so important. And don't forget your spouse's spiritual needs. Let your spouse know that you're praying for her or him. In fact, write out your prayer on your beloved's behalf. This type of love note goes beyond the sentimental to the spiritual. It goes a long way toward knitting your souls together—the deepest form of romance.

3. "HANG" TOGETHER.

Spend time together as a couple. It's too easy, as time passes, to find separate friends and separate interests and to spend more time apart. Hang out with your spouse. Don't just live together, *play* together. Find a project and work on it as a team. My wife and I just completed a remodeling project in our home. And yes, after putting in new carpet, hardwood floors, and wallpaper, we're still speaking to each other! It was hard work, but it was a blast.

This applies to the simple things too. Gas up the car, go to the car wash, or rake leaves *together*. Romance doesn't happen just in the bedroom. It starts wherever you're together.

4. PRAY TOGETHER.

Many men can't figure out why I include prayer in a list of suggestions for better romance. But if you pay attention, guys, you'll understand. Hearing your name on the lips of your spouse in prayer is very affirming and comforting. Couples who pray together are more in touch with each others' feelings and struggles and, as a result, are closer. Many men don't realize the deep longing women have for their husbands to pray with them and be the spiritual priest of their home. Prayer brings us into intimate contact with Almighty God and strengthens the intimate bond between husband and wife.

5. HAVE AN AFFAIR WITH YOUR SPOUSE.

What do people do when they're having an "affair"? There are secret rendevous, flowers, gifts, and lots of attention. People on the rebound of divorce often lose weight, spice up their wardrobe, and get a new hairstyle in hopes of getting back into the dating scene. Why don't people do these things when they're married?

Have an affair with your mate. Buy the sexy lingerie and try the new hairdo for your spouse. Don't wait for your anniversary or a birthday to do something special for your husband or wife. From time to time, bring home flowers or have a tub of hot, sudsy water waiting or buy a "thinking of you" card "just 'cuz." No special occasion, "just 'cuz" you love your spouse and want to show it. Spontaneous expressions of love and caring are often remembered the longest and are a great way to bring the flames of romance into a relationship that has gotten a little chilly.

And by all means, plan for time for just the two of you. Weekly or monthly, arrange for a sitter and go on a romantic date with your mate. Reconnect, talk, break the routine, and recommit your love to each other. If you learn a few simple ways to "seduce" your spouse, you'll do a lot to "affair-proof" your marriage.

Suzette and I left our honeymoon hotel a little more than ten hours ago. The kids are back and the routine awaits us. But the honeymoon doesn't have to be over. There's still some Martinelli's Sparkling Cider and cheesecake left. And tonight, when we're alone again, we'll sip the cider, eat the cheesecake, pray, and choose to keep the romance alive. It won't happen without some effort and creativity, but we're definitely worth it.

---

1. Ed Young, *Romancing the Home* (Nashville: Broadman & Holman Publishers, 1993), 9.
2. Philippians 2:3, 4.
3. *The Living Bible.*

Ways to Live With an Unbelieving Spouse

Hallmark® has seen to it that we pay homage to love and romance every February, so I'll oblige by looking at a situation that affects thousands of marriages—Christians married to unbelievers. A letter from a reader revealed a situation that confronts many every day.

Dear Randy, I am married and have two grown sons. I am the only one in my family who lives as a Christian. There are so many times when I just don't know what God would have me do, though I believe He wants me to stay in the marriage (we've been married 33 years). I joined the church four years ago. My husband also joined, but almost as soon as he did, he started falling away. It's almost like Satan roped him in and will not let go. He wants me to go to a New Year's Day party—football and fish fry. There will be drinking. I feel that I will be uncomfortable there, and I'm not sure what God wants me to do.

How are conflicts like this resolved? Can we go to the Word of God

5 Steps to Christlike Living

and find practical guidelines on how to live with an unbelieving spouse? I believe we can. God's Word "is useful for teaching, rebuking, correcting and training in righteousness."[1] We can trust it to be a source of wisdom regarding the problems we face in life.

Before we look at what God's Word says, however, let me state that I am not a marriage counselor. Never having gone through what the letter writer describes, I wanted the pointers in this chapter to be credible and to represent the viewpoint of someone who has "been there." So in preparing my response I consulted with a dear friend who lived in a spiritually divided marriage for many years. Her counsel is reflected in some of the tips I will share.

1. STAY IN THE MARRIAGE.

The writer of the letter says that she believes God wants her to stay in the marriage. The apostle Paul supports her belief.

> If a woman has a husband who is not a believer and he is willing to live with her, she must not divorce him. For the unbelieving husband has been sanctified through his wife, and the unbelieving wife has been sanctified through her believing husband. . . . God has called us to live in peace.[2]

God is not in the business of breaking up families. The letter writer was married some 29 years before joining the church—a decision she and her husband made together. One partner remained strong in the Lord; the other has drifted back into the old lifestyle. This is definitely *not* a case of a believer deliberately entering into the "unequally yoked" situation that Paul instructed Christians to avoid.[3] But even if it were, Paul upheld the sanctity of the marriage commitment and saw the possibility of redemption for the unbelieving spouse through the spouse who is following Christ.

If you're in this situation and your spouse is willing to remain married, do not consider divorce an option. Stay in the marriage, and show your spouse the love of God.

2. PICK YOUR BATTLES PRAYERFULLY.

Don't be a martyr on every point of conflict that arises in your marriage. Pray first and then ask "What would Jesus do?" In the case of the New Year's party, consider going with your husband—*but don't drink!* You don't have to compromise principle to make your husband happy, and both are important.

Here is where a lot of Christians get messed up in their thinking. Jesus did not associate only with the spiritual community. *Wherever the need was greatest, Jesus was there.* When the Pharisees and teachers of the law learned of the banquet that Levi Matthew—a tax collector—was giving in honor of Jesus, they complained to the disciples, " 'Why do you eat and drink with tax collectors and "sinners"?' " Jesus answered them, " 'It is not the healthy who need a doctor, but the sick. I have not come to call the righteous, but sinners to repentance.' "[4]

Many Christians think that they must isolate themselves from those who are living a different lifestyle than theirs. They feel that all their friends must be Christians like themselves so they can avoid coming into contact with "sin." But what was our Lord's example?

> Jesus sat as an honored guest at the table of the publicans, by His sympathy and social kindliness showing that He recognized the dignity of humanity; and men longed to become worthy of His confidence. Upon their thirsty hearts His words fell with blessed, life-giving power. New impulses were awakened, and the possibility of a new life opened to these outcasts of society.[5]

Non-Christian social gatherings may be exactly where God wants to use you to represent the Christian lifestyle.[6] Your abstinence from alcohol, foul language, questionable jokes, etc., may elicit a comment or question from someone at the party, giving you an opportunity to witness for your Lord.

In the meantime, your presence at the party says to your mate, "I'm here because of you. This event is important to you, therefore it is important to me." Your spouse already knows that you'd rather not be there. But your willingness to put his or her needs ahead of your own comfort will be appreciated. And perhaps if you do this for your spouse, your spouse will go with you to church from time to time.

Remember—the more things you can do to help strengthen the marriage, the better. Your unbelieving spouse is watching everything you—the Christian—do. It is vitally important that your spouse see that your commitment to God makes you a better wife or husband.

3. DEVELOP A SUPPORT GROUP.

Surround yourself with Christian friends who will provide the spiritual nurture and encouragement you're not getting at home. If your spouse doesn't object, invite your Christian friends over and have potluck dinners in your home. Don't force your spouse to join, but make sure he or she is welcomed in the group. This type of gathering will provide opportunities for your spouse to associate with believers and to ask questions. And the strength you derive from those who share your faith will buoy your spirits during those times when you battle loneliness.

4. DON'T NAG.

Some Christians feel that the way to "save" their unbelieving spouses is to nag them into the kingdom of heaven. They're at the church every time the door opens. They leave Christian literature around the house, preach at their spouses about their failure to come with them to church, and lay heavy guilt trips on them about their smoking, drinking, card playing, etc. This is not the way Jesus won people's hearts.

Again, Paul said, "Do not allow what you consider good to be spoken of as evil," and "If it is possible, as far as it depends on you, live at peace with everyone."[7] Don't use your church attendance or prayer life as a club with which to beat your spouse. If you do, your Christianity will become loathsome to your spouse. Do your best to live at peace with your spouse, and let the Holy Spirit do the convicting. He's better at it than you are.

5. USE COMMON SENSE.

Common sense is not so common, but trust God to guide you in this situation. Certainly, if you're in an abusive situation or you or your children are at risk because of your faith, separation may be wise. God would not frown on this. And not every unbelieving spouse will want to remain in a marriage that is divided spiritually. Paul said that you are not bound if the unbelieving partner leaves.[8] The point is, *don't you be the one to chase your spouse away!* "How do you know, wife, whether you will save your husband? Or, how do you know, husband, whether you will save your wife?"[9]

Use that principle I discussed in the previous chapter—the one about out-serving your spouse. Make a conscious effort to put your spouse's needs first, and pray that God will soften your spouse's heart as he or she reaps the benefit of your commitment to Christ.

Living in a spiritually divided marriage isn't easy. You will have challenges to face. But it need not be an intolerable situation either. If you will follow your Master's example, you, too, may bring to your spouse the water of life.

---

1. 2 Timothy 3:16.
2. 2 Corinthians 7:13, 15.
3. See 2 Corinthians 6:14.
4. Luke 5:30-32.
5. Ellen G. White, *The Desire of Ages* (Nampa, Idaho: Pacific Press, 1940), 274.
6. See Matthew 5:14.
7. Romans 14:16; 12:18.
8. See 1 Corinthians 7:15.
9. Verse 16.

Ways to Live With a Believing Spouse

Back when these chapters were articles in *Signs of the Times,* my editor (Marvin Moore) suggested that I follow up my "Unbelieving Spouse" article with one showing the flip-side—living with a *believing* spouse. Once I had retrieved my jaw from the floor, we discussed the possibilities of looking at this issue from the unbelieving (or at least unchurched) partner's perspective.

How do you get along in a spiritually divided home? Your spouse is a dedicated Christian. Church and spiritual activities hold deep meaning for him or her. You, however, don't share a similar commitment. Perhaps you "believe" in your own quiet way, but organized religion is not your thing. Or maybe your situation bears resemblance to the following story contributed by a friend and coworker of mine:

Larry and Leona married very young: she was 15 and he was 23. Leona was a devoted Christian—to a fault. A firm believer. Larry was also a believer but never found it necessary to be baptized. Larry had been to every evangelistic meeting that ever came to the church. He probably knew the Bible as well as—and maybe even better than—Leona did. He was a good person. He always treated people nicely and fairly. He had a pleasant spirit and was a bit of a tease.

Leona, on the other hand, was a "serious" Christian. For some reason she felt it necessary to remind Larry of everything he did that didn't fit her definition of "correct" Christian living. One summer day, for example, Larry had been in the field all morning and most of the afternoon and had missed his lunch. He hurried into the house to make a sandwich and planned to head right back into the field. When Leona saw him slapping his sandwich together and getting ready to take a bite, she blurted out "You know, Larry, you really should wash your hands and then ask the Lord to bless your food before you eat it." Leona was always good at reminding folk about things like getting to church on time, praying before going to sleep, skirts that were too short, and immodest necklines.[1]

Sound familiar? If this hits painfully close to home, gently recommend that your spouse read the previous chapter. In the meantime, here are a few suggestions on how to live in peace with your believing spouse.

1. TALK ABOUT IT.

Suppose your spouse came home one evening and announced plans to quit his or her job and start a home-based business. Would that announcement be important enough to cause you to turn off the TV and talk? I bet it would. I'm guessing you'd want to know what circumstances led your spouse to make this decision. You'd probably want to know why he or she felt this was the right thing to do and what impact this decision would make on the family. You might also want to know more about this home-based business. What is it? What's involved in getting it started? How much capital is needed up front to get it going? What are the pros and cons of pursuing this venture?

A commitment by one's spouse to follow Jesus Christ is no less

5 Steps to Christlike Living

worthy of discussion. It is a life-changing decision that goes deeper than weekly church attendance. If your spouse has experienced something the Bible refers to as being "born again," he or she will be a different person. People who become Christians experience changes in everything from their language to their circle of friends. Activities they once enjoyed will no longer attract them. And things they used to have no time for, or even ridiculed (like going to church), will suddenly become important.

The growth of the love of God in your spouse's heart can be a blessing to your marriage and household. But you do need to talk about it. Don't let religion come between you and your spouse, causing you to live two separate lives like enemies forced to share the same foxhole. Anything this important in the life of your spouse deserves discussion. You owe it to yourself to become knowledgeable about the commitment your mate has made. Why does he or she think this is the right thing to do. What will be his or her level of commitment to the church and to you? Where do you fit in?

2. SET YOUR BOUNDARIES.

Once you've taken the time to discover what your spouse's faith entails, establish some boundaries. Be supportive of your spouse's decisions, but remind him or her that your religious convictions are up to you alone. This may prevent the kind of scene described in the story above. Christians may be well-meaning in their attempts to get their spouses on "the straight and narrow," but in their enthusiasm they may use tactics that resemble nagging or shaming. (Refer your spouse to step #4 in last month's article.)

You do have a right to your own convictions. Be open to discussion, but ask your spouse to give you space to work through your thoughts on points of religious belief and practice.

3. GO TO CHURCH.

Accompany your spouse to church occasionally. I know this may sound like a lot to ask, but it isn't really if you love your spouse. A favorite author of mine said something quite to the point:

It's easy for us to forget that whenever we show we care for someone, we're changing our behavior to meet their needs. A husband may change his normal route home from work to buy flowers for his wife. A wife may change her plans so she can cheer her husband at his softball game. When your spouse asks you to change your behavior to accommodate him or her, your spouse is simply keeping you up to date on the latest emotional needs. He or she is asking for your care. [2]

Again, anything important to your spouse should be important to you. Meet some of the people with whom your spouse associates at church. Learn who the pastor is, and hear what your spouse is being taught from week to week. This "sacrifice" will keep you involved in this important part of your spouse's life, and it will give you opportunities to express love in ways that have meaning to your beloved.

4. DON'T PERSECUTE

I know of many situations in which unbelieving spouses take great delight in engaging in behavior designed to make their Christian mates uncomfortable. This is selfishness, not love. Last month, I warned believing spouses not to nag. Christians should not judge, accuse, preach at, or lay guilt trips on their unbelieving mates. Similarly, unbelievers shouldn't make life miserable for their mates just because they follow Christ. My grandfather never joined the church, but he respected my grandmother's faith and never tried to prevent her from praying, contributing money, or attending church. He knew his smoking and drinking made her uncomfortable, and so he enjoyed these personal pleasures outside of the home.

The point is, do your best to live at peace with your spouse. Learn to give and take—*and do more giving than taking!*

5. TAKE OWNERSHIP OF YOUR OWN SPIRITUALITY.

Whether or not you're a churchgoer, spirituality is an important aspect of life. It is just as important as your health and shouldn't be left to chance. Do you know what you *do* believe in? Rocker legend Bob

5 Steps to Christlike Living

Dylan recorded a song entitled "Gotta Serve Somebody." He was absolutely right; everyone believes in something. Even atheists believe; they believe that God doesn't exist. That position requires as much faith as the opposite belief.

So take ownership of your own spirituality by investigating your beliefs and making solid choices based on your discoveries. Ask questions. Quiz your spouse on his or her beliefs. Read some books. Include the Bible in your search, beginning with the Gospel of John. Keep a journal of your questions and reactions as you read, and then share your observations with your spouse or with a clergyperson. Get solid information, then make a clearheaded, well-thought-out decision about your own relationship to Christ.

As I said at the conclusion of the previous chapter, living in a spiritually divided marriage isn't easy. You will have challenges to face. But it need not be an intolerable situation either. Talk it out, set your boundaries, show love, make your marriage a "persecution-free" zone, and take control of your own spirituality. If you do this, you'll avoid a "Larry and Leona" household.

---

1. I'm indebted to Naomi Babb for this story. The names Larry and Leona are fictional.

2. Willard F. Harley, Ph.D., "Let's Get Real," *Homes of Honor*, holiday 1998, p. 10.

Ways to Get Along With Your Teenager

Somewhere around here I have a contract my oldest daughter signed when she was 11 or 12, promising her mother and me that she would not drive us crazy when she became a teenager. Candice will turn 18 this year (2001). Where *is* that contract? I want it—*now!*

Bill Cosby was right when he said that babies are guilty of false advertising. You bring home this tiny bundle of baby-powdered wonder and marvel over every gurgle, coo, and burp—only to have that same child grumble, sass, and dump all over you fourteen or so years later. The sweet little hair bows they glue onto the hairless domes of folliclely-challenged baby girls? *False advertising!* The way babies squeal, kick, and rotate their arms like windmills in a hurricane when they see you? *False advertising!* The little crumb snatchers who steal your heart when they're small enough to fit in the palm of your hand grow up, sometimes breaking your heart in the process.

But teenagers can be a lot of fun too. With a little laughter, grace, and a *lot* of prayer, you can survive and even thrive during the teen years. Here are a few suggestions.

5 Steps to Christlike Living

1. LIGHTEN UP.

You needn't consider every conflict with your teenagers a cosmic battle between the forces of good and evil upon which the destiny of the universe depends. Give your teens room to make some of their own choices. And choose your battles wisely. As long as no one is bleeding, I'm usually satisfied.

And keep a good sense of humor. I remember teaching Candice how to drive a car with a manual transmission. Now *that* was funny! Believe me, there are plenty of times when things get "heavy," so seize the moments to laugh together. Remember, when it comes to teens, "a cheerful heart is good medicine."[1]

2. ADMIT MISTAKES.

Saying "I'm sorry" when we blow it is never easy. Saying it to our teens is even harder. Why? Pride. As parents, we want to be "right." To always be in control and never surrender the reins of authority. Consequently, often when we have a conniption, we force our children to live with the consequences even when we know we're in the wrong.

Clear the air. If you're wrong, admit it to your teen and ask forgiveness. And be specific. Don't just say "I'm sorry," tell your teen what you're sorry for. Say "It was wrong for me to scream at the top of my lungs like a maniac. I was out of control, and I apologize." Such apologies fulfill the Bible admonition to "confess your sins to each other."[2]

3. BE CONSISTENT, FIRM, AND FAIR.

Set fair boundaries, and be consistent in how you enforce them. Once a rule is established, get your teen to "sign on" and agree to it. Suzette and I occasionally call a family council to discuss a rule we're wanting to implement. After spelling out the whys and wherefores, we open the floor for discussion. Once we're satisfied that the rule is reasonable and understandable, we move forward with everyone's agreement. This makes enforcement easier, and no one can say, "You never said that before!"

Sometimes, it's hard to be consistent. My resolve tends to weaken in the face of tears and pouting. But Suzette—a.k.a. "The Terminator"—

keeps me from caving in and reminds me that we need to present a united front. This is very important. Children do try to play one parent against the other. Don't fall for it. Agree ahead of time to back each other up. And follow through on what you say. This helps children learn that Mom and Dad say what they mean and mean what they say.

4. KEEP TALKING.

Teenagers are bundles of emotion. Especially is this true for teenage girls. The drama, mood swings, and emotional outbursts drive me crazy! One minute they're as silent as the stone statues on Easter Island; the next they're trying to climb in your lap and cuddle like a two-year-old. Face it. The teen years are like a roller-coaster ride. *Hang on, scream, and be prepared to stare death in the face!* But whatever you do, keep talking. Even if you have trouble understanding each other, keep the lines of communication open. Ask about the algebra test coming up. Keep up with the latest gossip within your child's circle of friends. And be sure you make time for them to talk with you.

If your teen gets moody and doesn't want to talk, give him or her some room to be alone—for a while. But don't let silence go unchallenged for long periods. Get in there and get them talking. Make sure they know that no subject is off limits. This will make it easier for your teen to open up about serious subjects such as sex and drugs. And don't fail to talk up what your teen does right. Compliment their choice in clothes (if you can), and praise their accomplishments.

5. PRAY, PRAY, PRAY!

Did I mention Pray? Teens have a way of bringing you to your knees. That's OK! We're never stronger than when we're on our knees, helpless before God. You will often find your authority challenged, your judgment questioned, and your instructions ignored. You need to pray. Pray for wisdom to know how to parent the child you've been given.[3]

And here's a shocker, *keep praying with your teenager.*

I know what you're saying: "My teenager? Pray? With *me?*" Yes. I haven't lost my mind. Pray with your teenager. When the kids are small, prayers and worship time come easily. Something changes, though, as

5 Steps to Christlike Living

they grow. When they start driving, earning their own money, going out with their friends, etc., they start to establish their own identity and seem to be less interested in spiritual things. But this is precisely why and when we need to keep their spiritual connection to God strong by continuing to pray with them.

For a while, Suzette and I stopped "tucking Candice in" with prayers at bedtime. She was hitting that teenage coolness, and we didn't press the issue. However, we began feeling that we were abdicating our responsibility of keeping spiritual things in front of our daughter, so we began inviting her into our room for prayers at night. Candice was reluctant at first, coming more out of a sense of duty than delight. But then something wonderful happened. The first night we missed inviting her in for prayers, she came in on her own and asked, "Aren't we going to have prayer?" Suzette and I smiled at each other and breathed a prayer of thanks for what God was doing through this simple act of devotion.

These five suggestions may not smooth your way with your teenager. Some children have deep-seated psychological problems. Divorce, abuse, neglect, and violence leave deep emotional scars. A child with a substance-abuse or anger problem or with A.D.D. may be turning your home into a war zone. In cases of serious rebellion, you may need to seek professional help from Christian counselors, gather some trusted friends to pray for your family, and even take the serious step of temporarily removing the child from the home. Whatever you do, though, give the outcome—and your child—to God, asking Him to hold your family in His arms as you ride through the storm.

I'm very proud of our teenager. She drives me crazy but still thinks her parents are kinda cool and worth listening to. And we think she's pretty cool too—most of the time. Now, if I could just find that contract . . . !

---

1. Proverbs 17:22.
2. James 5:16.
3. James 1:5.

CHRISTIAN LIVING

The final seven chapters deal with a variety of "basic training" essentials for the Christian. How to experience salvation, how to study the Bible, belief in God, getting more from church, etc., are some of the basics covered in this section.

Of special importance (to me anyway) is the chapter on reaching out to members of different ethnic groups. Some Christians only allow their religion to take them so far. When it comes to confronting prejudice, their religion comes up short. If we are going to truly live like Christ, our faith must be more than "skin deep." This chapter provides some practical advice on how to stretch beyond our comfort zones to embrace people who may be different from us.

Finally, the last chapter on how to stop being miserable, ends on a high note of escaping the attitudes that keep us from living life to the fullest. Enjoy.

Steps to Salvation

I was eleven the day I almost drowned. A "harmless" prank at a summer-camp swimming pool nearly ruined my day—and my life!

I was away from home for the first time at Camp Cedar Falls, in Southern California's San Bernardino mountains. A swim in the camp pool with my friends seemed like the perfect way to terrorize the girls and cool off at the same time. There was only one small problem. I couldn't swim. Not to worry. I was secure in the water as long as my feet could touch the bottom of the pool.

The sun was warm, the girls were squealing, and the water felt great as the boys from cabin Fox kept things interesting in the pool. About the time we were running out of energy, my best friend suggested that I try a dive on the other side of the rope. Now, I knew that the rope was the dividing line between the shallow and deep ends of the pool, but my friend was insistent that I could still touch the bottom just this side of that rope.

My resistance weakened under a barrage of coaxing that included dares and all the pride-wounding pressures 11-year-old boys level at

5 Steps to Christlike Living

each other. Eventually convincing myself that I'd still be able to touch bottom, I took the plunge on the other side of the rope—the side that, up until then, I had *always* avoided.

The dive was fine. I began to surface and stretched my feet downward in search of the pool floor. *It wasn't there!* Instant panic washed over me like the six-foot-deep waters I began thrashing against. I struggled to get my head above the water so I could cry out to my friend who was standing only a few feet away on the side of the pool, but I couldn't. What was worse, I could see him laughing at my antics, apparently unaware of the danger I was in.

Again, I fought against the water with all my might. Frolicking swimmers were all around me, but no one was paying any attention; they had no idea I was drowning. Just as my strength was beginning to fade, my friend's expression suddenly became dead serious. It dawned on him that I really was in trouble. He immediately jumped in and was at my side in seconds. In my desperation I seized him around the neck and nearly took us both down, but he managed to get us safely to the side.

My friend pulled me to safety that day, but he wasn't alone. God was in that pool too. It was Him whom I thanked over and over again that night as I breathed ragged prayers of gratitude for saving my life.

Have you been saved? No, I'm not talking about being saved from drowning. I'm talking about being saved from sin. Have you wondered how to move from a mere intellectual belief in Jesus Christ to a saving relationship with Him in which you experience forgiveness for the mistakes of your past and you receive the gift of eternal life? I'd like to share with you five steps you can take today that will bring salvation within your reach.

1. RECOGNIZE YOUR NEED OF HELP.

The Bible describes the human condition like this: " 'There is no one righteous, not even one; there is no one who understands, no one who seeks God. All have turned away, they have together become worthless; there is no one who does good, not even one.' . . . For all have sinned and fall short of the glory of God."[1]

The sin problem is universal. No one is exempt. Every man, woman, boy, and girl is infected with the sin virus—a virus that is 100 percent lethal. "For the wages of sin is death."[2] The first step toward salvation from this desperate situation is to recognize that you are a sinner and that it is impossible for you, in your own strength, to resist the power of evil or to save yourself from its fatal results.

2. UNDERSTAND THAT GOD LOVES YOU AND WANTS TO SAVE YOU.

Many people have grown up with the idea that God is some sort of cosmic cop waiting to catch them in sin so He can condemn them to the horrors of hell. Nothing could be farther from the truth. God is " 'compassionate and gracious . . . , slow to anger, abounding in love and faithfulness, maintaining love to thousands, and forgiving wickedness, rebellion and sin.' "[3]

God does not want to punish us. Instead, " 'God so loved the world that he gave his one and only Son, that whoever believes in him shall not perish but have eternal life. For God did not send his Son into the world to condemn the world, but to save the world through him.' "[4]

It's true that God hates sin. Why wouldn't He? Sin is a killer. It separates us from God,[5] cutting us off from the source of life. He hates sin but loves sinners—you and me. But because He is also a God of justice, He must punish sin. It is here that the glory of the salvation plan becomes clear.

3. LOOK TO JESUS.

Just as I needed a savior that day in the swimming pool, we humans needed Someone to come and save us from drowning in sin. That Savior came in the person of the God-Man Jesus Christ. Jesus came to reveal the love of the Father and to be our sin-bearer. He bore the punishment for our sins upon the cross. "Surely he took up our infirmities and carried our sorrows. . . . He was pierced for our transgressions, he was crushed for our iniquities; the punishment that brought us peace was upon him, and by his wounds we are healed."[6]

One of my favorite devotional writers put it this way:

5 Steps to Christlike Living

Christ was treated as we deserve, that we might be treated as He deserves. He was condemned for our sins, in which He had no share, that we might be justified by His righteousness, in which we had no share. He suffered the death which was ours, that we might receive the life which was His.[7]

4. BELIEVE.

As you look at the Savior dying on the cross and realize that He suffered that agony so you could be saved, you begin to understand the ugliness of sin and want to be forgiven, cleansed, and set free. You confess your wretchedness to God, and you repent—in other words, you turn away from those things that separate you from Him. As you do this, you accept God's promise to "forgive us our sins and purify us from all unrighteousness."[8]

You cannot atone for your past sins; you cannot change your heart and make yourself holy. But God promises to do all this for you through Christ. You believe that promise. You confess your sins and give yourself to God. You will to serve Him. Just as surely as you do this, God will fulfill His word to you. If you believe the promise—believe that you are forgiven and cleansed—God supplies the fact; you are made whole, just as Christ gave the paralytic power to walk when the man believed that he was healed. It is so if you believe it.[9]

The criterion for salvation hasn't changed. "Believe in the Lord Jesus, and you will be saved."[10]

5. RECEIVE THE GIFT OF ETERNAL LIFE.

If I hadn't accepted my friend's help when he jumped in to save me, I would have drowned. Similarly, each of us must accept Christ as our Savior or His gracious act on the cross will not benefit us. Potentially life-saving medicine does no good while it's in the bottle. The sick person must *receive* the pills into his or her body in order to be cured.

Trust Christ *alone* to save you. Neither good works nor being religious can save you. "It is by grace you have been saved, through faith—and this not from yourselves, it is the gift of God."[11] Christ and Christ *alone* can atone for your sins and make you clean before God. Go to Him in prayer right now and tell Him that you are ready to receive His perfect life in place of your sinful one. Confess your sins and claim the promise that "to all who received him, to those who believed in his name, he gave the right to become children of God." "And this is the testimony: God has given us eternal life, and this life is in his Son. He who has the Son has life."[12]

I still thank God for saving me. I thank Him for saving me from drowning that day in the pool, and I thank Him for saving my soul.

Why not let Him save you too?

---

1. Romans 3:10-12, 23.

2. Romans 6:23.

3. Exodus 34:6, 7; see also Ezekiel 33:11.

4. John 3:16, 17.

5. See Isaiah 59:2.

6. Isaiah 53:4, 5.

7. Ellen G. White, *The Desire of Ages* (Nampa, Idaho: Pacific Press® Publishing Association, 1940), 25.

8. 1 John 1:9.

9. Ellen G. White, *Steps to Christ* (Hagerstown, Md.: Review and Herald Publishing Association, 1977), 50.

10. Acts 16:31.

11. Ephesians 2:8.

12. John 1:12; 1 John 5:11, 12.

Tips for Getting More out of Church

Not long ago I was sitting in church, listening to the pastor go through the always-too-long list of announcements, when something amusing happened. He asked one of the worship leaders to make a special announcement. The woman he called on had been sitting on the edge of her seat, poised like a cat, ready to pounce on the microphone the second she was given the chance. Now that her moment had come, she sprang into action. Her smile was wide, her eyes danced, and her whole body literally vibrated with enthusiasm.

What's she so excited about? I wondered, my curiosity now properly piqued.

"Ladies, it's our turn," she began. "We're going to have a *tea . . .*" I kinda blacked out at that point. *Ugh!* I groaned inwardly. Though the event was not for me (thank goodness!), I couldn't help but think, *Could there be anything on God's green earth* more *boring?*

Forgive me, ladies. I know guys just don't "get it." But I pictured a roomful of women with lace doilies, tea cups, and finger food all around, and I mentally gagged. I just couldn't imagine anyone wanting to spend

CHRISTIAN LIVING

their Sunday afternoon like that. Surely there was a lawn to mow or a golf game on TV or a tooth that needed pulling. . . . But a *tea?*

Ever feel that way about church itself? Like you'd rather spend the day in bed or cleaning out the garage than to go hear another boring sermon? Sadly, many Christians, especially men, can identify. I've heard more than one male friend of mine say that if it weren't for the example he wanted to set for his children, he wouldn't bother. And the most often stated reason for the feelings of these men? Because they don't "get much out of it."

For others, the reasons might include a long list of "if onlys." *If only* the choir sang better. *If only* the organist didn't play so loud. *If only* we went back to singing from the hymnal like we used to in the good ol' days and got rid of the "praise team" and their song slides. *If only* we could bring in drama teams and a big-screen TV with surround sound. *If only* the preacher would stick to three points and get his sermon time down to 20 minutes—30 minutes tops. *If only* the pews were cushioned or the PA system were better or the church weren't so crowded or . . .

You get the point.

At the risk of irritating my fledgling—but hopefully growing—readership, let me suggest that if you identify with any of the above remarks, the problem may not be with your church. It may be with you, with your understanding of what church is all about.

Church is not a place of entertainment—a place where the "audience" files in and sits with arms folded and facial expressions that say to the pastor and other "performers" up front, "Bless me—I dare you!" Church is first and foremost a place of *worship.* Jesus said, "My house is the house of prayer,"[1] not an amusement park. Church is not a place we come to *get* but to *give:* our praise, our adoration, our thanks, our testimony, our concerns, our lives in joyful service to God and to each other. The question "What's in it for me?" is misguided and reveals a consumer mindset masquerading as Christianity.[2]

But, for the sake of argument, let's say that you really aren't after entertainment; you just want the richest possible experience at church. Let me offer you five tips.

5 Steps to Christlike Living

1. PRAY MORE.

I don't mean in the clichéd sense of "just pray about it." No, I'm being very practical here. Start the night *before* you go to church. Pray that God will speak to you personally through the sermon, the music, the Bible study, or some aspect of the service. Pray that the pastor will be free in the Holy Spirit—free from fear, insecurity, or distraction—so that God's Word will come through bold, clear, timely, effective, and redemptive. Pray that your attitude will be right. Pray that your fellow worshipers will receive the touch from God they need. And pray that someone will give his or her heart to Jesus.

2. COME WITH AN OFFERING OF THANKSGIVING AND PRAISE.

Did you notice how many items in my list of "if onlys" were related to God? That's right: None. Zero. That's because we've allowed "worship" to become so horizontally focused. It's all about what *we* want, what keeps *us* happy. Whatever you want to call that, don't call it worship—because it isn't. Worship is ascribing worth or value to *God*. The psalmist said, "Enter his gates with thanksgiving and his courts with praise."[3] People who truly worship don't come to church to make themselves happy; they come because they love God and want to make Him happy with their offerings of praise and thanksgiving.

Before going to church, prepare a list of at least ten things you can praise God for. Take the list with you to church, and when it's time for the main prayer, instead of nodding off while the elder drones on, pull out your list and offer a sacrifice of praise to God for how good He's been to you.

Praise brings God's presence,[4] and "in [His] presence is fullness of joy."[5] Give God your praise, your love, your worship, and stop worrying about all that horizontal stuff. Get your eyes on Jesus. Get "vertical."

3. SIT CLOSER TO THE FRONT.

Why do church folk always race for the back pews? The back seats are the noncommittal seats. The back pews are for the detached, the uninvolved, the uninitiated, for those who aren't that interested in what's going on. This is true in the classroom as well as in the corporate committee room. (There are exceptions, of course. People with young children often sit near the back to keep a fussy baby or fidgety toddler from disturbing the service.)

If you sit in the back, you're more likely to be distracted by who is coming in the door, what people are wearing, how loud the teenagers or toddlers are, etc. *Move forward.* Get close to the action. Seat yourself where distractions are minimal and you can see better, hear better, and receive the blessing God wants to give you.

4. TAKE NOTES.

Don't just sit there waiting to be spoon-fed. Bring your Bible to church. Turn to and underline passages referred to in the sermon. Write down the main points of the message on a note pad or on a blank page of the bulletin for future reference. Doing so will keep your mind engaged in the message and improve your ability to "hear" God speaking to you through the voice of your pastor.

5. COME SEEKING TO GIVE A BLESSING RATHER THAN TO GET ONE.

Ask God to make you aware of someone who may need a hug, a pat on the back, a word of encouragement, or a prayer. Don't be content to leave the service until you've made someone's trip to church that day worthwhile. This—and not plush carpet, great sound systems, or state-of-the-art, computerized, multimedia presentations—is what church is all about.

The law of God's kingdom is that you lose to win, serve to become great, give in order to receive. Jesus said, "Whoever wants to save his life will lose it, but whoever loses his life for me will find it."[6] In other words, if you put your life—your needs, desires, tastes, preferences, etc.—first, you'll always lose. You'll always be spiritually empty and discontent. But if you'll put the needs and desires of others ahead of your own, you'll find life—the life of joy, the life of abundance, the life of Christ—right there in church.

5 Steps to Christlike Living

And when you do, even that ladies' tea won't sound so bad.
Nah!

---

1. Luke 19:46, KJV.

2. This is not to say that there aren't some truly boring church services. There's no virtue in a service devoid of life, energy, and joy. But do what you can to put yourself in a proper attitude for worship and let God take care of the rest.

3. Psalm 100:4.

4. See Psalm 22:3; 2 Chronicles 5:11-14.

5. Psalm 16:11, KJV.

6. Matthew 16:25.

Things You Can Do to Support Your Pastor

Imagine that you are a trained professional with years of schooling—perhaps even a Ph.D.—and years of practical, on-the-job experience. Now picture everyone from the delivery person to the 80-year-old great-grandmother of one of your best clients telling you how to do your job.

How would it feel to have your motives, lifestyle, and integrity questioned by those you serve? How would you react to having your competency and job performance constantly assailed by people who had absolutely zero training in your field? And what if you were expected to be on call 24 hours a day to provide comfort and counsel to these same people while never being able to have a problem yourself? Sound like a tough job?

Welcome to the world of the pastor. Pastors are supposed to be perfect in every way: great speakers, theologians, counselors, administrators, and evangelists—and perfect spouses and parents to boot. But, as the following statistics from a 1991 survey of pastors conducted by Fuller Institute reveal, the stress of the job takes an enormous toll:

90 percent of pastors work more than 46 hours a week.

80 percent believe pastoral ministry has affected their families negatively.

33 percent say that being in the ministry is an outright hazard to their family.

75 percent report a significant stress-related crisis at least once in their ministry.

50 percent feel unable to meet the needs of the job.

90 percent feel they were inadequately trained to cope with ministry demands.

70 percent say they have a lower self-image than when they started in the ministry.

40 percent report a serious conflict with a parishioner at least once a month.

33 percent confess involvement in some inappropriate sexual behavior with someone in the church.

70 percent have no close friends.[1]

You may have never guessed that your pastor struggled with feelings of loneliness, inadequacy, and depression. But now you know—so what can you do about it?

1. CALL A MORATORIUM ON CRITICISM.

Get control of your tongue. The apostle James accurately depicts the power of the tongue and the pain it can produce: "All kinds of animals, birds, reptiles and creatures of the sea are being tamed and have been tamed by man, but no man can tame the tongue. It is a restless evil, full of deadly poison. With the tongue we praise our Lord and Father, and with it we curse men, who have been made in God's likeness. Out of the same mouth come praise and cursing. My brothers, this should not be."[2]

Determine you won't use your tongue to tear down your pastor. Look for ways and words to build up and encourage your shepherd. If you have a legitimate beef, then talk directly to the pastor and avoid spreading the seeds of your discontent among other members. They can't help the situation, and your criticism will only breed a spirit of negativism in the church. Follow Paul's admonition to "not let any un-wholesome talk come out of your mouths, but only what is helpful for building others up according to their needs, that it may benefit those who listen."[3]

2. PRAY FOR AND WITH YOUR PASTOR.

Instead of criticizing your pastor, pray for and with him or her. Pastors are special targets of the enemy. Discouragement is Satan's number one weapon against God's spiritual leaders. We can support our pastors by praying specifically for God to protect and bless them in several key areas:

• Humility—Ask God to give your pastor a servant's heart and a teachable spirit.

• Wisdom—Pray that your pastor will be sensitive to God's leading, able to discern His plans and purposes.

• Health—Ask God to place a hedge of protection around your pastor, keeping him or her safe when traveling and in good health.

• Family—Pray for the pastor's relationships with his or her spouse and children. Pray that the pastor will make the needs of his or her family second only to God.

• Time—Pray that the demands of ministry, such as counseling, committee meetings, visitation, and sermon preparation won't overshadow the time your leader needs to spend alone with God.

• Integrity and anointing—Pray that your pastor will maintain his or her integrity in all circumstances. Pray for the anointing of the Holy Spirit on his or her ministry.

Besides praying *for* your pastor, consider praying *with* your pastor. Last year I asked my pastor if I could serve him by being his personal prayer partner. He eagerly accepted this offer of spiritual support and friendship. When our busy schedules allow, we get together once a week to share joys and disappointments, prayer requests, and the dreams and frustrations of ministry.

5 Steps to Christlike Living

If you would like to become your pastor's prayer partner, I strongly recommend you get the book *Partners in Prayer*, by John Maxwell (no relation). This book will tell you step by step how to be a partner in prayer with your pastor.

3. SEND YOUR PASTOR CARDS OR NOTES OF APPRECIATION.

I saw a survey on what motivates employees to perform their best. It said, to my surprise, that appreciation was a better motivation than money. Your pastor is accustomed to getting blasted for things he or she did or said or didn't do or say. Surprise your pastor by sending a card that tells him you're praying for him. Acknowledge the spiritual gifts you see manifested in your pastor, and let her know how her ministry has blessed you. Let your pastor know you appreciate the sacrifices he or she is making to follow God's call.

4. TAKE THE KIDS.

You will endear your pastor and his or her spouse to you forever by volunteering to keep their kids for a few hours so they can spend time alone with each other. Ministry often stresses marriage. The spouse of the leader experiences the same microscope of parishioner scrutiny as his or her mate does, and pastoral spouses often have to play second-, third-, fourth-, or fifteenth-fiddle to the needs of others. Call the pastor and ask him or her to get out the calendar and pick a date when you will babysit the kids so they can go out on a date. Your pastor will rise up and call you blessed!

5. SEND YOUR PASTOR ON A RETREAT.

During a six-month period when our church was between pastors, my wife and I served as interim pastoral couple. By the end of those six months, we were physically and emotionally exhausted. The church showed its appreciation and love to us by sending us on an all-expense-paid weekend in nearby Sun Valley, Idaho. We still talk about that weekend as one of the most refreshing getaways we've ever had.

Pool your resources with several other members and send your pastor and family away for a weekend retreat where they can rest, play, and get away from the demands of ministry for a while. They'll never forget your kindness.

Loving and supporting your pastor is both a privilege and a practical fulfillment of the golden rule. You will be blessed as you minister to the one who ministers to you. And the benefits you and your church will receive from an encouraged, prayed for, rested, and appreciated pastor will be too many to count.

---

1. John Maxwell, *Partners in Prayer* (Nashville, Tennessee: Thomas Nelson Publishers, 1996), 80.

2. James 3:7-10.

3. Ephesians 4:29.

Ways to Reach Out to Members of a Different Ethnic Group

I remember clearly the first time I entered the Fred Meyer store in Nampa, Idaho. My wife, Suzette, and I had just flown in from Los Angeles at the invitation of Pacific Press® Publishing Association, the company I now work for. I had been offered a job as an assistant book editor, and Suzette and I had come to Idaho to explore housing possibilities.

I left Suzette in the motel room with a sinus headache and drove to the Fred Meyer store in search of some over-the-counter relief. I wasn't in the store long before I felt eyes boring into the back of my neck. I couldn't help notice how many shoppers were noticing me. Then I realized that I was the only person of color in the store. Instantly, I felt conspicuous—as though someone had turned a spotlight on me. And though no one mistreated me in any way, I wasn't sure I could get used to this type of celebrity.

I don't mind telling you that I wrestled long and hard with the Lord about my call to Idaho. Was the job going to be worth the discomfort of trying to fit into a community where we were such an obvious minority?

CHRISTIAN LIVING

That first shopping trip to Fred Meyer occurred more than a dozen years ago, and (at this writing) we still live in Nampa—with no regrets. God has wonderfully blessed. He called us to be missionaries in a culture that is very different from our own. Why? To stretch us beyond our comfort zones in areas of faith and fellowship and to do the same for those in this fairly homogenous community.

What about the church? It's been said that eleven o'clock on Sunday morning is the most segregated hour of the week. And though I am a Seventh-day Adventist Christian and worship on Saturday, the same could be said of my denomination as well. When it comes to racism, prejudice, and discrimination, the church has failed to differ substantially from the world.

In 2 Corinthians 5:16, Paul states his position clearly: "From now on we regard no one from a worldly point of view." In the world, people are divided along lines of skin color, gender, economic status, language, etc. But in the church of Christ, we "are all sons of God through faith in Christ Jesus. . . . There is neither Jew nor Greek, slave nor free, male nor female, for you are all one in Christ Jesus."[1]

Would you like to know how to begin reaching out to members of other ethnic groups? Let me suggest five simple ways to get started.

1. BEGIN TO EXPLORE.

How many people unlike yourself form your inner circle? How willing are you to cross over into unfamiliar territory and develop a friendship with somebody who is different? Take steps to enter someone else's world. Go home with them after church. Get on their turf. Visit places where you might not be comfortable but where you can see how your friend lives and what his or her world is like.

2. READ LITERATURE OR VIEW FILMS ABOUT AND BY MEMBERS OF OTHER ETHNIC GROUPS.

Gary is one of my closest friends. When my family moved to Idaho, he and his family showed an immediate interest in us. Our daughters became fast friends and remain so to this day. Gary wanted to know about Black heritage and wanted insight into some of the struggles of our people. Our talks were often frank and pointed. But it wasn't until he bought the six-part video documentary series called *Eyes on the Prize: America's Civil Rights Years, 1954–1965* and watched it with his children that he began to understand the struggle and pain of African-Americans. With tears in his eyes, my friend embraced me and committed himself to the ministry of reconciliation that God gave the church.

This ministry begins with understanding. Visit the library. Get your hands on literature from other ethnic groups. Get a fresh perspective on the passions, experiences, struggles, and dreams of those outside your own circle. As you do this, walls of ignorance and misunderstanding will begin to crumble. (For suggestions on where to start, see "Recommended Resources.")

3. BRING IN SPEAKERS OF DIFFERENT ETHNIC BACKGROUNDS.

It is not uncommon in large urban centers for churches of different cultural backgrounds to have no interaction whatsoever—even when they are of the same denomination! Believe me when I tell you I've visited cities where the members of one church have never darkened the doorway of another church that is only a few blocks away. These churches preach the same doctrine, pray to the same God, and pay tithe to the same institutional storehouse. But the cultural divide prevents them from enjoying fellowship with each other.

One way to break through this barrier is to encourage your pastor to arrange a pulpit swap with the pastor of a church of another ethnic makeup. Hold joint services that involve different worship styles. Allow yourself to be blessed by the nuances and fresh perspectives the other group brings to your understanding of God. Get out of your "box" and rub shoulders with these other members of the body of Christ. It'll change you.

4. JOIN TOGETHER FOR PRAYER.

Many churches have begun to come together for what is called a "concert of prayer." The idea is for churches within a city or geographical area to conduct joint prayer meetings for the purpose of seeking revival in their churches and communities. A few years ago I spoke at a city-wide prayer conference in Memphis, Tennessee, in which several Black churches came together and committed themselves to this concert-of-prayer model. When I suggested including the White churches, the idea was met with great skepticism. The Black pastors had little confidence that their White counterparts would be willing to participate in a program that was initiated by non-Whites. We prayed about it. Approximately six months later I encountered one of the Black pastors from Memphis. He told me that the concert of prayer was convening monthly, and that new churches—including White churches—were joining the effort. If we can just start praying together, there is no force on earth that can prevent God's people from being united.

5. TAKE THE INITIATIVE.

I tell my audiences, "Don't wait for someone else to initiate the friendship. If the Spirit is telling you to reconcile, then reconcile. If the Spirit says make a new friend, then make a new friend. Take that first step. Just move!"

Be assured that the enemy wants to keep Christians weak and divided. Is it easier to stay within our own comfort zones? You bet. Is it hard work to enter into the world of other people and to try to see life from their perspective? Yes. Is it difficult to develop long-term friendships with someone of a different ethnic group? Perhaps. But is it the will of God that we love one another as Christ has loved us? Yes. In fact, it is our Savior's command.[2]

In the process of establishing new friendships, be honest. Don't be phoney. Ask real questions. Risk appearing stupid. Be willing to hear the good, the bad, and the ugly things that have transpired between members of different cultural groups. Face your own prejudices and then honestly confess them to God and to your neighbor who may need to hear that confession. Study the Scripture together, and look for opportunities—such as festivals or performances—that celebrate your cultures.

Upon our arrival in Idaho, I told my wife that we could endure our White neighbors' stares because they didn't know anything about us.

5 Steps to Christlike Living

Our task would be to let them get to know us and to see the kind of people we are—that we share the same hopes, aspirations, and dreams for our children as they do for theirs. Today I believe we've made a difference and helped build some bridges of understanding in our community.

Is it perfect? What society on earth is? But I'm determined to live out the principles and values of the kingdom of heaven—where, because of Jesus, my true citizenship resides.

How about you?

---

1. Galatians 3:26, 28; see also Ephesians 2:14-22.
2. See John 15:12, 17.

Recommended Resources

Tony Evans. *Let's Get to Know Each Other.* Nashville: Thomas Nelson Publishers, 1995.

Make Us One. Delbert W. Baker, ed. Nampa, Idaho: Pacific Press®, 1995.

John Dawson. *Healing America's Wounds.* Ventura, California: Regal Books, 1994.

Eyes on the Prize: America's Civil Rights Years, 1954–1965 (six-part documentary video series). Boston: Blackside, Inc., 1986.

Eyes on the Prize II: America on Racial Crossroads, 1965–1985 (eight-part documentary video series). Boston: Blackside, Inc., 1989.

Face to Face: Seeking Racial Reconciliation (video). Madison: InterVarsity Christian Fellowship, 1990.

Tips for Getting More out of Bible Study

Did you know that the average American household has between three and seven Bibles? It's true! We are a Bible-saturated society. More than three hundred English translations of the entire Bible exist today—even one in *Pig Latin!* You would think that with all these Bibles we'd be very knowledgeable about God and the basics of the Christian faith, right? *Wrong!*

A 1991 Gallup poll revealed that despite the widespread and continuing popularity of religion in America, there is "a glaring lack of knowledge about the Bible, basic doctrines, and the traditions of one's own church." This lack of basic Bible knowledge results in inconsistencies and overlapping of beliefs. "People tend to choose the items of belief that best suit them. Reginald Bibby, Canadian sociologist, calls this 'religion a la carte.' Substantial proportions of traditional Christians, for example, subscribe to non-Christian beliefs and practices, such as reincarnation, channeling, astrology, and fortune telling."[1]

Why this appalling superficiality of faith and lack of knowledge when Bibles are in abundance? Because we're not taking the time to

5 Steps to Christlike Living

read the Bibles we have. At the frantic pace at which we live our lives today, we manage only a surface knowledge of the Bible and become superficial Christians in the process.

What's the answer? How can we get more depth, more meaning, out of God's Word?

1. SET A GOAL.

If you consider God's Word important, you will set some realistic and measurable goals for acquainting yourself with it. Rather than setting a time-oriented goal such as "I will read the Bible for 15 minutes every day," try establishing a reading goal. Read at least one complete chapter from the Bible every day, and keep your reading confined to one book at a time. In other words, read the book of John, or Acts, or Genesis, etc., one chapter a day. I find that this is a good way to grasp the overall meaning of that particular author and book of the Bible. Some Bible reading plans call for reading a chapter from the New Testament, one from the Old Testament, and something from Psalms or Proverbs. If that works for you, go for it. I find this a bit distracting; jumping back and forth makes me lose the continuity of what I'm learning.

Your goal doesn't have to include starting with Genesis. You've probably tried reading the Bible all the way through from the beginning and gotten bogged down somewhere around Leviticus or in the "begats." This is only one way to read the Bible. Start where your interest lies. Want to know more about Jesus? Read the book of John or one of the other Gospels. Interested in prophecy? Start with Daniel or Revelation. Read Acts to learn more about the early church, or Genesis to learn about creation and the origin of life. One chapter a day will not take huge amounts of time and will help you establish a habit of reading God's Word daily.

2. JOURNAL SCRIPTURE.

As you read, keep a pad and pencil handy and "journal" your thoughts about certain passages that interest, inspire, convict, or impress you. For instance, suppose you're reading the eighth chapter of Mark and you come across the following conversation between Jesus and His disciples:

Jesus and his disciples went on to the villages around Caesarea Philippi. On the way he asked them, "Who do people say I am?"

They replied, "Some say John the Baptist; others say Elijah; and still others, one of the prophets."

"But what about you?" he asked. "Who do you say I am?"

Peter answered, "You are the Christ."[2]

Stop reading for a moment and answer Jesus' question "Who do you say I am?" as if He were talking to you. Write your answer on your pad. This is "journaling" the Scripture. It's nothing more complex than reacting on paper to what you read in the Bible.

Experiment with journaling for a moment using the following text:

He (God) Himself has said, I will not in any way fail you nor give you up nor leave you without support. [I will] not, [I will] not, [I will] not in any degree leave you helpless, nor forsake nor let [you] down, [relax My hold on you].—Assuredly not![3]

Get some paper and simply write your response to what God has just said to you in this text.

You will find that journaling makes the Word of God real and personal. Stopping to write your feelings and reactions to the passages that impress you will do more for you than would just reading words and mechanically pressing on toward your goal of reading a chapter a day. It will make the Word of God come alive in your experience. It will help you to know and love God more—which is the purpose of studying the Bible in the first place.

3. MEMORIZE.

David said, "I have hidden your word in my heart that I might not sin against you."[4] "Hiding" the Word of God in our hearts means committing Scripture to memory. David discovered that familiarity with God's Word deters sin, and memorizing Scripture is an excellent way to familiarize yourself with God's Word.

5 Steps to Christlike Living

One way to get started is to write down key passages on index cards. Carry a card or two with you in your shirt pocket or purse and read them periodically throughout the day until you can repeat the verses by heart. Start now. Try the verse I just mentioned, "I have hidden your word in my heart that I might not sin against you." Write this on a three-by-five card or a Post-It note, and carry it with you today. Read it at least three times today, and see if you've got it "hidden" in your heart by the time you go to bed. Not only is this practice a deterrent against sin, it will retrain your brain to think God's thoughts and to recognize and appreciate God's values.

4. USE THE JOURNALISTIC QUESTIONS.

To go deeper than just a surface reading of the Bible, apply the journalistic questions—Who? What? When? Where? and Why?—to the chapter you're reading. (This technique works for either solo or group study.) First, pray for the Holy Spirit to show you something important to your spiritual growth in the chapter you've chosen to study, then read through the chapter without stopping. Next, starting at the beginning of the chapter, ask the five journalistic questions as you read each verse. While some of the questions won't fit every verse, this exercise will help you visualize the setting and imagine what it would have been like to be there. Asking these questions also uncovers totally new insights into passages you thought you already knew well.

To get started, try this technique with the following stories: blind Bartimaeus (Mark 10:46-52); Zacchaeus (Luke 19:1-10); the feeding of the five thousand (John 6:1-15); and Jesus' appearance to the disciples on the road to Emmaus (Luke 24:13-35). When you've completed the exercise, pray, asking God to help you see what meaning the insights you've gained have for your own life and how you can apply them. If you're studying by yourself, write out your answer. If you're studying with a group, discuss the insights and applications. In either case, pray about your discoveries.

5. JUST DO IT.

If the slogan "Just do it!" is good enough for Nike, it's even more appropriate for Bible students. Don't just read the Word and go about business as usual. *Do it.* Put it into practice.

At a recent Essence Awards program, gospel artist Kirk Franklin observed, "We write songs that degrade our women and praise God for the awards we win. . . . It's time we stopped preaching Christ and started walking Christ." Franklin was saying that profession without practice is meaningless. Hearing or reading without doing is equally empty.

"Do not merely listen to the word, and so deceive yourselves," wrote James. "Do what it says."[5] You'll fall into the worst kind of deception if you don't act on what God is saying to you. Think of all the sermons you've heard, Bible study classes you've attended, and religious tapes you've listened to over the years. If Christians acted on one-third of all they've heard, our churches and the world would be radically different places!

Do you want to know God better through His Word and get more out of Bible study? Set a goal, journal Scripture, commit Scripture to memory, use the journalistic questions, and then act on what you read. You've got nothing to lose and everything to gain. Start today.

---

1. George Gallup, Jr., *Poll Releases*, April 2, 1999: "Easter Draws Americans Back to Church." Internet: <www.gallup.com/poll/releases/pr990402b.asp>.

2. Mark 8:27-29.

3. Hebrews 13:5, Amplified.

4. Psalm 119:11.

5. James 1:22.

Reasons Why I Believe in God

Seat 14B. The business-class piece of cloth, foam, and metal on the top deck of a Boeing 747 was to be my "home" for the next twelve hours. My body was feeling the effects of giving 14 presentations in seven days in time zones that were 16 and 18 hours ahead of my own. Now that I was finished and bound for home, all I wanted to do was sink into that airline recliner, shut the world out with my headphones, and be left alone. But then there was Richard in 14A.

Richard was an older gentleman, somewhat gruff in appearance. His face and hands were leathery from years of hard work in the sun. He too, was returning home, and despite his gruff exterior, he was talkative—*very* talkative. And the last thing I wanted to do right then was talk.

For the next few hours we talked about his home in New Zealand, his outspoken views on politics that got him into trouble occasionally, and his career in farming. And as the miles of ocean passed thirty thousand feet below us, Richard kept talking *and* ordering booze. Since he was from the California wine country, Richard fancied himself an expert and wanted to compare New Zealand wines to the California brands he knew. *Great,* I thought. *This guy's gonna get plastered, and I'm going to bear the brunt of his behavior. Why me, Lord?*

Soon the answer became apparent.

Though I would rather have just withdrawn into a nonverbal cocoon of peace and quiet, I prayed that God would allow me to say a word on His behalf to my companion in 14A. I asked for the courage to witness and share my faith, and before long Richard inquired about my work.

My answer that I was an author of Christian books and worked for a publishing company that produced religious materials sparked a rather lengthy interchange on the existence of God. Richard was of the strong opinion that there was no God. The conversation was intense but not unpleasant. It forced me to do some serious thinking about my own convictions on this important subject. Why *do* I believe in God?

Let me share with you five of the reasons why I do believe.

1. THE PRESENCE OF DESIGN IN THE UNIVERSE.

William Paley was an English theologian and moral philosopher during the 18th century. He is famous for his "Divine Watchmaker" argument in favor of the existence of God. His supposition was that if you encountered a rock while walking, you might not stop to question who made the rock. But if instead you encountered a watch, you would conclude that it could not have come about by chance but that it was the product of some intelligent design. Human life and this world are far more intricate than a watch. Seasons, tides, gravity, the atmosphere, DNA, the eye—these all reflect intelligent design. I believe God is the Source of that intelligent design.

To update Paley's argument, I asked Richard to consider the aircraft we were sitting in. Six million parts and 171 miles (274 km) of wiring go into making a 747. I asked Richard to imagine those six million parts unassembled in a Boeing factory somewhere and then the factory exploding, sending those millions of parts high into the air. "What are the chances of those parts falling to earth in the precise order to form a perfectly assembled 747 aircraft?" I asked him.

5 Steps to Christlike Living

The odds of such a thing happening are inconceivable. A machine as complex as a commercial aircraft has form, function, and design. Therefore, even if nothing was known about the existence of the Boeing company, rational people would conclude that someone designed and built this aircraft. It didn't "just happen."

The universe, and especially our world, also has form, function, and design. To believe that our world—with its complex, yet perfectly balanced ecosystems—resulted from an "explosion" of matter and gasses in space requires an even greater stretch of the imagination than the 747 scenario. And even if you believe in the "Big Bang," you still have to solve the problem of who or what started the "Big Bang."

If there is design, there must be a designer.

2. THE EXISTENCE OF LOVE.

If there is no God, why then the existence of love? Love is illogical and unnecessary in a world created by chaos, chance, and evolution. Cells divide and multiply without love. Animals mate and bear their young without love. Trees bear fruit, bees pollinate flowers, grass grows, and eggs hatch without love. From a purely biological standpoint, love is not necessary for survival of the species.

Humans, likewise, do not need love in order to survive biologically, and yet we do love . . . and hate and dream and inspire. Why?

"God is love" said the apostle John.[1] God created human beings to be like Himself, "in his own image."[2] There is no other reason for love to exist. Because it does, I believe the God of love must also exist.

3. THE EXISTENCE OF MORALITY.

It is interesting to note that basic moral laws exist in all societies whether primitive or sophisticated. These universally observed prohibitions cover at least three basic forms of activity: murder, theft, and rape. Humankind, like the world it occupies, functions in a framework of order. Though statue law and common law may vary from culture to culture, these all have their roots in moral law, which provides the backdrop for all orderly behavior of humankind. Where does this universal consistency come from?

Again, cell division and biology occur without values, ethics, or morality. Why then do we have such things? Only humans understand the concept of right and wrong, good and evil. I believe God created a moral "compass" within the human heart. There is no other reason for morality to exist.

4. THE BIBLE.

The Holy Scriptures themselves bear witness to divine origin. Not that God wrote the words Himself, but "men spoke from God as they were carried along by the Holy Spirit."[3] This incredible Book has more than forty authors who wrote over a period of some fifteen hundred years! And yet there is a remarkable consistency from beginning to end.

Fulfilled prophecies verify the Scripture's reliability. Daniel, who lived six hundred years before Christ, accurately predicted the world powers of Babylon, Persia, Greece, and Rome! And the accuracy with which the Bible both describes and explains the human condition reveals a supernatural authorship. I believe that Author to be God.

5. MY EXPERIENCE.

Finally, I believe in God because of what He's done in my life. God talks to me, and I talk to Him. In thousands of ways that go beyond audible speech, God communicates His love for me. Through the Bible, nature, music, relationships, circumstances, and the inner witness of the Holy Spirit through the "still, small voice," God speaks and I hear.

Through Calvary's cross, God saves me and reveals His character of love. Lewis Sperry Chafer wrote, "Anyone can devise a plan by which good people go to heaven. Only God can devise a plan whereby sinners, [who] are His enemies, can go to heaven." I have peace, joy, confidence for the future, and hope for today because I believe He lives and loves me.

And should my belief ultimately prove to be wrong, what have I lost? I will live out my years happy, fulfilled, aspiring to benefit my fellow human beings, and making a positive difference in the world around me. Should atheists be proven wrong, however, they will have lost the privilege of knowing unconditional Love, and they will have surrendered the right to eternal life that belief in the Son of God provides. They will have exchanged seventy or so years for eternity—a billionaire's fortune exchanged for a quarter!

Richard and I left that plane friends rather than bitter enemies. No, he didn't "convert" and become a believer. But he did invite me to send him some of what I've written. I'm happy to do so. I love making new friends and introducing them to my best Friend, Jesus.

Seat 14A. Was my encounter with Richard just an accident? Chance? I choose to believe our meeting was—like life—by *design*.

---

1. 1 John 4:8.
2. Genesis 1:27.
3. 2 Peter 1:21.

Ways to Stop Being Miserable

A wise man once said, "There is a time for everything, and a season for every activity under heaven: a time to be born and a time to die, a time to plant and a time to uproot, . . . a time to tear down and a time to build, . . ."[1] To this venerable list I shall add: a time to start a book and a time to end a book.

Guess what time it is.

Over the past 20 or so chapters, we've talked about prayer, spiritual passion, reaching out to different ethnic groups, romance, being free in Jesus, guilt, living with teenagers, and getting more out of church. I thought long and hard about the topic for this last chapter, and I finally decided that I wanted to write about misery.

The words "miserable Christian" should be an oxymoron, like "jumbo shrimp," "working vacation," or "airline food." The two concepts don't go together. And yet, too many believers in Jesus are among the "frozen chosen," "walking wounded," and "holy hostages."

Here then, is my parting gift to anyone who yearns to leave the

5 Steps to Christlike Living

aforementioned group of sanctified sad-sacks: Five ways to stop being miserable.

1. START LOOKING FORWARD.

The most miserable people on earth are those who have a crook in their necks from constantly looking back over their shoulders at some past hurt. This is known as self-pity. Ask people why they no longer go to church, and nine times out of ten you'll hear a story of something that happened *years* ago that hurt their feelings.

Time marches on, but some people—even Christians who follow a Savior who gives them new life through a spiritual re-birth[2]—tenaciously cling to old wounds and harbor old grudges. Let them go! Life is not lived in the past. Stop rubbernecking and keep your eyes on Jesus, "the author and perfecter of our faith."[3] You'll never know what God has in store for you today and tomorrow if you keep focusing on yesterday. Like Paul, forget what is behind and press on toward the goal to win the prize for which God has called you.[4]

2. PRAY FOR GOD TO CHANGE YOU—NOT OTHERS.

A sure-fire recipe for misery includes plenty of prayer for God to change other people. You know the people I'm talking about, don't you? The boss who drives you crazy; the coworker who stabs you in the back; the church member who irritates your very soul. You pray and pray for God to do something in their lives to make them more lovable (or move them to another state), and there they remain like barnacles on a ship's hull, planted firmly in the way of your happiness and sucking the joy right out of you.

Want to escape the misery? Stop trying to change others. Pray instead for God to change *you.*

In her book *"Lord, Change Me,"* Evelyn Christenson wrote,

> I have discovered through the years that surprising things happen when I pray "Lord, change *me*—don't change my husband, don't change my children, don't change my pastor, change *me!*" This doesn't mean that I approve or even condone every-

124

thing they do, but rather that I concentrate on how *I* handle my actions and reactions. More and more the fact comes into focus that they, and not I, are responsible before God for their actions, but I am responsible for the changes that need to be made in *me*.[5]

Irritating people and circumstances will always be there. God will see to it that they're there for you. Because He's mean? Just the opposite. He knows you need them to help you grow to be more like Jesus. Take Evelyn's challenge and begin to pray differently. Ask God to change you, and see what happens.

3. ACCEPT RESPONSIBILITY FOR YOUR OWN ACTIONS.

Turn to any radio or TV talk show, read the newspaper, or sit in a Bible study group, and you will hear people blaming everybody and everything for what they've become. No one in this country wants to accept responsibility for his or her actions. The sugar in our Twinkies, the girlfriend who says No, the Prozac for our depression, the government, our parents, the butler, El Niño—you name it! We are the way we are because somebody or something made us this way.

I have been frustrated as I've sat in Bible study groups and listened week after week to individuals who have latched onto pop psychology's "diagnosis" of what ails them emotionally but won't move on to recovery with God. It seems that once some people know *why* they behave or respond a certain way, they have a justification for their actions and are content to rehearse forever the circumstances that brought them to this place. This is another way of "looking back" as described in point one above. Accept responsibility for your own actions, and accept God's power to overcome even hereditary tendencies toward wrongdoing. Yes, God's grace is sufficient.[6]

4. KNOW GOD FOR YOURSELF.

Remember the parable Jesus told about the ten virgins? These ladies were in a bridal party. They took their lamps and went to meet the bridegroom. Five took oil in jars along with their lamps, and five took

5 Steps to Christlike Living

only their lamps. There was a delay, and all ten became drowsy and went to sleep. "At midnight the cry rang out: 'Here's the bridegroom! Come out to meet him!' Then all the virgins woke up and trimmed their lamps. The foolish ones said to the wise, 'Give us some of *your* oil; our lamps are going out.' "[7]

The oil in the parable represents the Holy Spirit. When the five foolish virgins noticed that their lamps were burning low, where did they turn for oil? Their fellow bridesmaids. They didn't know where to get oil for themselves, so they turned to the ones who had some.

Many Christians are miserable and stunted spiritually because they are always dependent on someone else for their growth in the Lord. Take ownership of your walk with God. Go to the Source—the Lord Jesus Christ—and get the "oil" of the Holy Spirit from Him as you spend time in the Word, in prayer, and in service to others. Don't be caught, as the five foolish virgins were, without knowing Christ for yourself.

5. TAKE RISKS.

I saw in a magazine a motivational poster that had a sailing ship on it. The caption read, "Ships are safe in the harbor. But that's not what ships were made for."

Life is short. Don't limit yourself. Ask big things of God, and watch for opportunities to stretch beyond your comfort zone. You are a child of God, and "all things are yours"[8]

Refuse to let Satan cheat you out of experiencing the fullness of your Christian inheritance because of fear—fear of failure, fear of rejection, fear of getting hurt, etc. "You did not receive a spirit that makes you a slave again to fear, but you received the Spirit of sonship. "[9]

A friend sent me the following in an email. I don't know who wrote it, but whoever it was described a great way to live.

> People are often unreasonable, illogical, and self-centered. *Forgive them anyway.*
>
> If you are kind, people may accuse you of selfish, ulterior motives. *Be kind anyway.*

CHRISTIAN LIVING

If you are successful, you will win some false friends and some true enemies. *Succeed anyway.*

If you are honest and frank, people may cheat you. *Be honest and frank anyway.*

What you spend years building someone could destroy overnight. *Build anyway.*

If you find serenity and happiness, they may be jealous. *Be happy anyway.*

The good you do today people will often forget tomorrow. *Do good anyway.*

Give the world the best you have, and it may never be enough. *Give the world the best you've got anyway.*

You see, in the final analysis, it is between you and God. It never was between you and them anyway.

A wise man once said, "There is a time for everything, and a season for every activity under heaven." Now is the time to say Farewell. Go with God. Be everything He created you to be. Rejoice in the Lord always, and again, I say rejoice.[10]

---

1. Ecclesiastes 3:1-3.
2. See 2 Corinthians 5:17.
3. Hebrews 12:2.
4. See Philippians 3:14.
5. Evelyn Christenson, *"Lord, Change Me!"* (Wheaton, Illinois: Victor Books, 1988), 13.
6. See 2 Corinthians 12:9.
7. Matthew 25:6-8, italics added.
8. 1Corinthians 3:21.
9. Romans 8:15.
10. See Philippians 4:4.
(*Visit Randy's Web site at* <www.TAGnet.org/ifmypeoplepray>.)

If you enjoyed this book, you'll enjoy these by the same author:

On Eagles' Wings

Randy Maxwell. Life can tend to weigh you down with worry, fear, and impatience. Jesus wants to help us get above our daily trials and claim victory over our difficulties. *On Eagles' Wings* offers a sensible nuts-and-bolts approach to daily Christian living that will inspire you to take action.

0-8163-1345-8. Paperback. US$4.99, Can$6.99.

If My People Pray

Randy Maxwell. What would happen in our homes, churches, and communities if we followed God's counsel in 2 Chronicles 7:14, humbled ourselves, and prayed? This book shows how to experience prayer as relationship, power, and the key to revival.

English, 0-8163-1246-X. Paperback. US$10.99, Can$15.99.
Spanish, 1-5755-4031-2. Paperback. US$6.99, Can$9.99.

Bring Back the Glory

Randy Maxwell. From the author of *If My People Pray* comes this stirring follow-up call to prayer, compassion, and brokenness as the way to a revival of true godliness in our lives and churches. The message is urgent, often confrontational, and straight from the heart. *Bring Back the Glory* is written for everyone who craves change and the reviving showers of blessing God longs to send—*now!*

English, 0-8163-1788-7. Paperback. US$12.99, Can$19.49.
Spanish, 0-8163-9438-5. Paperback. US$12.99, Can$19.49.

Order from your ABC by calling **1-800-765-6955**, or get online and shop our virtual store at <**www.adventistbookcenter.com**>.
• Read a chapter from your favorite book
• Order online
• Sign up for email notices on new products